Osho was born in Kuchwada, Madhya Pradesh, on 11 December 1931. Rebellious and independent from childhood, he insisted on experiencing the truth for himself rather than acquiring knowledge and beliefs given by others.

He attained 'enlightenment' at twenty-one, and went on to complete his academic studies. He spent several years teaching philosophy at the University of Jabalpur. Meanwhile, he travelled throughout India delivering talks and meeting people from all walks of life.

By the late 1960s, Osho had begun to develop his unique dynamic meditation techniques. He felt that modern man is so burdened with the archaic traditions of the past as well as the anxieties of modern-day living, that he must go through a deep cleansing process before he can hope to discover the thought-less, relaxed state of meditation.

In the early 1970s, the West first began to hear of Osho. By 1974, a commune had been established around him in Pune, and the trickle of visitors from the West soon became a flood. Osho spoke on every aspect of life, and on the development of human consciousness. Based on his own existential experience rather than on intellectual understanding, he distilled the essence of what is significant to the spiritual quest of contemporary man.

Osho left his body on 19 January 1990. His commune in India continues to attract thousands of international visitors who came to participate in its meditation, therapy and creative programmes, or to simply experience being in a 'Buddhafield'.

Osho's talks have been published in more than six hundred volumes, and translated into over thirty languages.

OTHER BOOKS BY OSHO IN PENGUIN

- *Life's Mysteries: An Introduction to the Teaching of Osho*
- *The Inner Journey: Spontaneous Talks Given by Osho to Disciples and Friends at a Meditation Camp in Ajol, Gujarat, in India*
- *Osho: New Man for the New Millennium*
- *Little Book of Osho*
- *The Essence of Yoga*

OSHO

Yoga
The Science of Living

PENGUIN BOOKS

Penguin Books India (P) Ltd., 11 Community Centre, Panchsheel Park, New Delhi 110 017 India
Penguin Books Ltd., 80 Strand, London WC2R 0RL, UK
Penguin Putnam Inc., 375 Hudson Street, New York, NY 10014, USA
Penguin Books Australia Ltd., 250 Camberwell Road, Camberwell, Victoria 3124, Australia
Penguin Books Canada Ltd., 10 Alcorn Avenue, Suite 300, Toronto, Ontario, M4V 3B2, Canada
Penguin Books (NZ) Ltd., Cnr Rosedale and Airborne Roads, Albany, Auckland, New Zealand

Published by Penguin Books India 2002
Copyright © Osho International Foundation 1977
OSHO is a registered trademark of Osho International Foundation, used under license.

10 9 8 7 6 5 4 3 2 1

For sale in South Asia only

Coordinated by Amano Manish

Typeset in *Sabon Roman* by SÜRYA, New Delhi
Printed at Saurabh Print-o-Pack, NOIDA

Contents

Introduction

ANCIENT THOUGH THE discipline of yoga is, it has a lot in common with the very contemporary Osho understanding of how to live to the optimum.

Both approaches are empirical, absolutely scientific. Inspired by visionaries, they share the rare capacity of bridging the gap between themselves and anyone who is looking for happiness, harmony and fulfilment.

We have all known moments here and there when those three states converge. Maybe while running or dancing; walking by the ocean, trekking on a mountain trail; making love or creating a new computer programme. The good news is that we don't have to work for them; they come out of the blue. The not-so-good news is that we can't hold onto them or reproduce those experiences at will. They leave in the same mysterious way that they have arrived. Memorable as they are, they seem fated to remain just that—vignettes stored in our memory bank that we can, at best, retrieve to mentally caress when mired in less inspired moments.

The science of yoga is a methodology to make the accidental an everyday reality.

While more and more people are taking up yoga, probably for the vast majority of them it is simply a way to keep fit, a 'spiritually correct sport'. Perhaps they are unaware that the postures they know as yoga are just a small part, the least important ingredient, of an entire recipe for living.

Yoga: The Science of Living redresses the balance, explaining in simple, lucid language, a step-by-step system that can be, literally, life-transforming.

The reader is taken by the hand and led through the process of how to transcend the body, then the mind and, finally, how to 'fall into your own being'.

Speaking of *balance*, that's exactly the Osho take on the most accurate translation of *sanyama*—which the whole system of yoga is about. It is not, as more traditional renderings would have it—and as some contemporary 'yogis' misunderstand it—control or discipline, but balance, in-tunement, being natural. According to Osho, the whole idea of control is unnatural, repressive and ego-strengthening, which makes it somewhat counter-productive when you realize that the ego is the very thing coming between you and your being in tune, being natural and living in balance.

Discipline *is* significant, is needed, but not the kind that is adopted, that is external to one's own inner inclinations. *That* can only be an imposition and will function as a block in one's growth. But there is a discipline that is the outcome, the flowering of an organic process. It grows out of a deep intimacy with one's body-mind; out of having worked *with*, rather than against oneself. It is a discipline not of controlling oneself but being more conscious of oneself—in thinking, in feeling, in doing.

This book, created from spontaneous talks, is not a commentary on a commentary of an ancient treatise. The insights on which it is based, which provide the élan vital behind the words you will read, are those of an awakened consciousness, free of bias or devotion to any dogma or lineage.

A second element which can transform merely interesting content into an existential taste of the subject, is the inclusion of questions from people of many different backgrounds who have in common the urge to know themselves more fully, to be themselves more consciously.

But self-exploration—and it takes an iconoclast to expose the fact—can become self-importance; can make us somewhat precious, seriously serious. And those attitudes, like being controlling, provide fodder for the pesky ego. Osho effectively sabotages all that by cutting a swath through our notions of spirituality, with an irreverent sense of humour and spiritually-incorrect joke-telling.

For example . . . Two Jewish women, Sarah and Amy, met after twenty years. They had been together in college and they had been great friends, but for twenty years they had not seen each other. They hugged each other; they kissed each other.

Sarah said, 'Amy, how have you been?'

'Just fine. It is good to see you. How has the world been treating you, Sarah?'

'Would you believe that when Harry and I got married, he took me to a honeymoon: three months in the Mediterranean and a month in Israel? What do you think of that?'

'Fantastic!' Amy said.

'We came back home and he showed me the new house that he bought for me—sixteen rooms, two swimming pools, a new Mercedes. What do you think of that, Amy?'

'Fantastic!'

'And now, for our twentieth anniversary, he gave me a diamond ring . . . ten carats.'

'Fantastic!'

'And now we are going to go on a cruise around the world.'

'Oh, that's *fantastic*!'

'Amy, I have been talking so fast about what Harry did and has been doing for me. I forgot to ask what your Abe has done for you.'

'Oh, we have had a good life together.'

'But what has he done special?'

'He sent me to charm school.'

'Sent you to charm school? What did you go to charm school for?'

'To learn how to say "fantastic" instead of "bullshit."'

Suddenly, self-discovery is revealed as fun and yoga is, well, simply *fantastic*.

In Osho's words:

That's all yoga is all about—to make you aware of the fantastic. It is right by the corner waiting for you, and you are drowned in bullshit. Unhook yourself, loosen yourself out of it. Enough is enough!

And this decision cannot be taken by anybody else. You have to decide. It is your decision the way you are. It is going to be your decision if you want to change and be transformed.

Life is fantastic; only that much can I say to you. It is just around you and you are missing it. There is no need to miss anymore.

And yoga is not a belief system. It is a methodology, a scientific methodology how to attain the fantastic.

Maneesha James

ॐ

1. Ask a Question Close to Home

Dharana, concentration, is confining the mind to the object being meditated upon.

Dhyan, contemplation, is the uninterrupted flow of the mind of the object.

Samadhi is when the mind becomes one with the object.

The three taken together—dharma, dhyan, and samadhi—constitute sanyama.

By mastering it, the light of higher consciousness.

ONCE A MASTER of Zen invited questions from his students. A student asked, 'What future rewards can be expected by those who strive diligently with their lessons?'

Answered the master, 'Ask a question close to home.'

A second student wanted to know, 'How can I prevent my past follies from rising up to accuse me?'

The master repeated, 'Ask a question close to home.'

A third student raised his hand to state, 'Sir, we do not understand what is meant by asking a question close to home.'

'To see far, first see near. Be mindful of the present moment, for it contains answers about future and past. What thought just crossed your mind? Are you now sitting before me with a relaxed or with a tense physical body? Do I now have your full or partial attention? Come close to home by asking questions such as these. Close questions lead to distant answers.'

This is the yoga attitude towards life. Yoga is not metaphysical. It does not bother about the distant questions—faraway questions, about past lives, future lives, heaven and hell, God, and things of that sort. Yoga is concerned with questions close at home. Closer the question, the more is the possibility to solve it. If you can ask the question closest to you, there is every possibility that just by asking, it will be solved. And once you solve the closest question, you have taken the first step. Then the pilgrimage begins. Then, by and by, you start solving those which are distant—but the whole yoga inquiry is to bring you close at home.

So, if you ask Patanjali about God, he won't answer. In fact, he will think you a little foolish. Yoga thinks all metaphysicians foolish; they are wasting their time about problems which cannot be solved because they are so far away. Better start from the point where you are. You can only start from where you are. Each real journey can begin only from where you are. Don't ask intellectual, metaphysical questions of the beyond: ask questions of the within.

This is the first thing to be understood about yoga: it is a science. It is very pragmatic, empirical. It fulfils all the criteria of science. In fact, what you call science is a little far away, because science concentrates on objects. And yoga says, unless you understand the subject, which is your nature, closest to you, how can you understand the object? If you don't know yourself, all else that you know is bound to be erroneous, because the base is missing. You are on faulty ground. If you are not enlightened within, whatsoever light you carry without is not going to help you. And if you carry the light within, then there is no fear: let there be darkness outside; your light will be enough for you. It will enlighten your path.

Metaphysics does not help; it confuses.

It happened. When I was a student in the university, I joined the subject of moral philosophy, ethics. I attended only the first lecture of the professor. I could not believe that a man can be so outdated. He was talking almost a hundred years back, as if he was completely unaware of what new growth has happened to the subject of moral philosophy. But that could have been forgiven. He was tremendously boring, as if he was making all efforts to bore you. But that was also not a big problem; I could have slept. But he was annoying also, jarring—his voice, his manners . . . But that, too, one can become accustomed to. He was very much confused. In fact, I have never come across a man with so many qualities all joined in one person.

I never went again to his class. Of course, he must have been annoyed by that, but he never said anything. He waited for his time, because he knew one day I will have to appear in the examination. I appeared. He was even more annoyed because I got 95 per cent marks. He could not believe it.

One day when I was coming out of the university cafeteria and he was going in, he caught hold of me. He stopped me and said, 'Listen. How did you manage? You only attended my first lecture, and for two years I have not seen your face. How did you manage to get 95 per cent marks?'

I said, 'It must be because of your first lecture.'

He looked puzzled. He said, 'My first lecture! Just out of one lecture? Don't try to befool me. Tell me the truth.'

I said, 'Propriety won't allow it.'

He said, 'Forget all about propriety. Just tell me the truth. I will not mind.'

I said, 'I have told you the truth, but you have misunderstood it. If I had not attended your lecture, I would have got 100 per cent. You confused me! That accounts for those 5 per cent I lost.'

Metaphysics, philosophy, all distant thinking simply confuse you. It leads you nowhere. It muddles your mind. It gives you more and more to think, and it doesn't help you to become more aware. Thinking is not going to help: only meditation can help. And the difference is: while you think, you are more concerned with thoughts; while you meditate, you are more concerned with the capacity of awareness.

Philosophy is concerned with the mind; yoga is concerned with consciousness. Mind is that of which you can become aware: you can look at your thinking, you can see your thoughts passing, you can see your feelings moving, you can see your dreams floating like clouds. Riverlike, they go on and on; it is a continuum. The one that can see this is consciousness.

The whole effort of yoga is to attain to that which cannot be reduced to an object, which remains irreducible, to be just your subjectivity. You cannot see it because it is the seer. You cannot catch hold of it, because all that you can catch hold of is not you. Just because you can catch hold of it, it has become separate from you. This consciousness, which is always elusive and always stands back and whatsoever effort you make, all efforts fail . . . to come to this consciousness—how to come to this consciousness—is what yoga is all about.

To be a yogi is to become what you can become. Yoga is the science of stilling what has to be stilled and alerting what can be alerted. Yoga is a science to divide that which is not you and that which is you, to come to a clear-cut division so that you can see yourself in pristine clarity. Once you have a glimpse of your nature, who you are, the whole world changes. Then you can live in the world, and the world will not distract you. Then nothing can distract you; you are centred. Then you can move anywhere you like and you remain unmoving, because you have reached and touched the eternal, which never moves, which is unchanging.

Today we start the third step of Patanjali's *Yoga Sutras*, 'Vibhuti Pada.' It is very significant because the last, the fourth, 'Kaivalya Pada,' will be just attaining to the fruit. This third 'Vibhuti Pada,' is the ultimate as far as means are concerned, techniques are concerned, methods are concerned. The fourth will be just the outcome of the whole effort. Kaivalya means aloneness, absolute freedom of being alone, no dependence on anybody, on anything—

so contented that you are more than enough. This is the goal of yoga. In the fourth part, we will be talking only about the fruits, but if you miss the third, you will not be able to understand the fourth. The third is the base.

If the fourth chapter of Patanjali's *Yoga Sutras* is destroyed, nothing is destroyed, because whosoever will be able to attain to the third, will attain to the fourth automatically. The fourth can be dropped. It is, in fact, in a way, unnecessary because it talks about the end, the goal. Anyone who follows the path, will reach to the goal, there is no need to talk about it. Patanjali talks about it to help you, because your mind would like to know, 'Where are you going? What is the goal?' Your mind would like to be convinced, and Patanjali does not believe in trust, in faith, in belief. He is a pure scientist. He simply gives a glimpse of the goal, but the whole basis, the whole fundamental basis is in the third.

Up to now we were getting ready for this 'Vibhuti Pada', the ultimate in means. Up to now in two chapters we have been discussing means which help, but those means were outer. Patanjali calls them *bahirang*, 'on the periphery'. Now these three—*dharana, dhyan, samadhi*—concentration, meditation, *samadhi*—these three he calls *antarang*, 'internal'. The first five prepare you, your body, your character—you on the periphery—so that you can move inwards. And Patanjali moves step by step: it is a gradual science. It is not a sudden enlightenment; it is a gradual path. Step by step he leads you.

ॐ

The first sutra:

> *Dharana, concentration, is confining the mind*
> *to the object being meditated upon.*

The object, the subject, and the beyond—these three have to be remembered. You look at me, I am the object; the one who is looking at me is the subject. And if you become a little more perceptive, you can see yourself looking at me, that is the beyond. You can see yourself looking at me. Just try. I am the object, you are looking at me. You are the subject who is looking at me. You can stand by the side, within yourself. You can see that you are looking at me. That is the beyond.

First, one has to concentrate on the object. Concentration means narrowing of the mind.

Ordinarily, mind is in a constant traffic—a thousand and one thoughts go on moving, like a crowd, a mob. With so many objects, you are confused, split. With so many objects, you are moving in all directions simultaneously. With so many objects, you are always, almost, in a state of insanity, as if you are being pulled from every direction and everything is incomplete. You go to the left, and something pulls you to the right; you go to the south, and something pulls you to the north. You are never going anywhere, just a muddled energy, a whirlpool, constant turmoil, anxiety.

This is the state of ordinary mind—so many objects that the subjectivity is almost covered by them. You cannot have a feel who you are, because you are so much concerned with so many things you don't have a gap to look into yourself. You don't have that stillness, that aloneness. You are always in a crowd. You cannot find a space, a corner, where you can slip into yourself. And the objects continuously asking for attention, every thought asking for attention, forcing exactly that the attention should be given to it. This is the ordinary state. This is almost insanity.

In fact, to divide mad people from non-mad people is not good. The distinction is only of degrees. It is not of quality: it is only of quantity. Maybe you are 99 per cent mad and he has gone beyond—a 101 per cent. Just watch yourself. Many times you also cross the boundary in anger, you become mad—you do things you cannot conceive of yourself doing. You do things for which you repent later on. You do things for which you say later on, 'I did it in spite of me.' You say, '. . . as if somebody forced me to do it, as if I was possessed. Some evil spirit, some devil forced me to do it. I never wanted to do it'. Many times you also cross the boundary, but you come back again and again to your normal state of madness.

Go and watch any madman. People are always afraid of watching a madman because, suddenly, watching a madman, you realize your own madness also. Immediately, it happens, because you can see at the most the difference is of degrees. He has gone a little ahead of you, but you are also following, you are also standing in the same queue.

William James once went to a madhouse, came back, became very sad, covered himself with a blanket. The wife could not understand. She said, 'Why are you looking so sad?' He was a happy man.

He said, 'I have been to the madhouse. Suddenly, the thought occurred that between these people and me, there seems to be not much difference. There is a difference, but not much. And sometimes I have also crossed the boundary. Sometimes in anger, sometimes in lust, sometimes in anxiety, depression. I have also crossed the boundary. The only difference seems to be that they are stuck and they cannot come back and I am still a little flexible and I can come back. But who knows? Someday, the flexibility may be lost. Watching those madmen in the madhouse, I became aware that they are my future. Hence, I am very much depressed. Because the way I am moving, sooner or later I will overreach them.'

Just watch yourself, and go and watch a madman; the madman goes on talking alone. You are also talking. You talk invisibly, not so loud, but if somebody watches you rightly, he can see the movement of your lips. Even if the lips are not moving, you are talking inside. A madman talks a little louder; you talk a little less loudly. The difference is of quantity. Who knows? Any day you can talk loudly. Just stand by the side of the road and watch people coming from office or going to office. Many of them, you will feel, are talking inside, making gestures.

Even people who are trying to help you— psychoanalysts, therapists—they are also in the same boat. In fact, more psychoanalysts become mad than do people of any other profession. No other profession can compete with psychoanalysts in going mad. It may be because living in close quarters with mad people, by and by, they also become *unafraid* of being mad; by and by, the gap is bridged.

I was reading an anecdote:

One man was attending his local doctor for an examination. 'Tell me, do you get spots before the eyes?' asked the doctor.

'Yes, doctor.'

'Frequent headaches?' asked the doctor.

'Yes,' said the patient.

'Pains in the back?'

'Yes, sir.'

'So do I,' declared the doctor. 'I wonder what the heck it can be.'

The doctor and the patient, they are all in the same boat. Nobody knows what the heck it can be.

In the East, we never created the profession of psychoanalysts, for a certain reason. We created a totally different type of man: the yogi. Not the therapist. The yogi is one who is qualitatively different from you. The psychoanalyst is one who is not qualitatively different from you. He is in the same boat; he is just like you. He is not different in any way. The only difference is that he knows about your madness and his madness more than you know. He is more informed about madness, about insanity, neurosis, psychosis. Intellectually, he knows much more about the normal state of human mind and humankind, but he is not different. And the yogi is totally a different man, qualitatively. He is out of the madness you are in: he has dropped that.

And the way in the West you are looking for causes, for ways and means how to help humanity, seems to have, from the very beginning, gone wrong. You are still looking for causes outside—and the causes are within. The causes are not outside, not in relationship, not in the world; they are deep in your unconsciousness. They are not in your thinking: they are not in your dreams. The analysis of dreams and the analysis of thoughts is not going to help much. At the most, it can make you normally abnormal, not more than that. The basic cause is that you are not aware of the traffic and the traffic noise of the mind, that you are not separate, distant, aloof—that you cannot stand as a witness, as a watcher on the hill. And once you look for a cause in a wrong direction, you can go on piling up case histories upon case histories, as it is happening in the West.

Psychoanalysis goes on piling up case histories upon case histories . . . and nothing seems to come out of it. You dig up the mountain, and not even a mouse is found. You dig up the whole mountain—nothing comes out of it. But you become experts in digging, and your life becomes an investment in it, so you go on finding rationalizations for it. Always remember, once you miss to look in the right direction, you can go on infinitely—you will never come back home.

It happened:

Two Irishmen landed in New York. They had not been around very much, so they decided to take a train trip. As they were riding along, a boy came, selling fruit. They recognized oranges and apples, but there was a strange fruit they had never seen before, so they asked the boy, 'What is that?'

He answered, 'That is a banana.'

'Is it good to eat?'

He said, 'Sure.' 'How do you eat it?' they asked.

The boy showed them how to peel a banana, so each bought one. One fellow took a bite of it, and just then the train went into a tunnel.

He said, 'Great heavens! Pat, if you haven't eaten the darn thing, don't do it! I ate mine, and I have gone blind!'

Coincidences are not causes: and the Western psychology

is looking into coincidences. Somebody is sad; you start immediately looking into coincidences *why* he is sad. There must have been something wrong in his childhood. There must have been something wrong in the way he was brought up. There must have been something wrong in the relationship between the child and the mother or the father. There must have been wrongs, something wrong in the environment. You are looking for coincidences.

Causes are within; coincidences without. That is the basic emphasis of yoga, that you are looking wrongly now, and you will not ever find real help. You are sad because you are not aware. You are unhappy because you are not aware. You are in misery because you don't know who you are. All else is just coincidence.

Look deep down. You are in misery because you have been missing yourself, you have not yet met yourself. And the first thing to be done is *dharana*. Too many objects are there in the mind; the mind is much too overcrowded. Drop those objects by and by; narrow down your mind; bring it to a point where only one object remains.

Have you ever concentrated on anything? Concentration means your whole mind is focused on one thing. On a rose flower. You have looked at a rose so many times, but you have never concentrated on a rose. If you concentrate on a rose, the rose becomes the whole world. Your mind becomes narrowed down, focused like a torchlight, and the rose becomes bigger and bigger and bigger. The rose was one in a million objects, then it was a very small thing. Now, it is the all, the whole.

If you can concentrate on a rose, the rose will reveal qualities that you have never seen before. It will reveal colours that you have been always missing. It will reveal to you fragrances that were always there but you were not sensitive enough to recognize them. If you concentrate totally, your nose is only filled with the fragrance of the rose—all else is excluded, only the rose is included in your consciousness, is allowed in. Everything excluded, the whole world drops out, only the rose becomes your world.

There is a beautiful story in Buddhist literature. Once Buddha said to his disciple, Sariputra, 'Concentrate on laughter.' He asked, 'For what am I to look into it?' Buddha said, 'You are not to look for anything specially. You simply concentrate on laughter, and whatsoever laughter reveals, you report.'

Sariputra reported. Never before and never after has anybody looked so deeply into laughter. Sariputra defined and categorized laughter into six categories. 'They are arranged in hierarchical fashion; from the most sublime to the most sensuous and unrefined.' Laughter revealed its inner being to Sariputra.

First he called *sita*, 'a faint, almost imperceptible smile manifest in the subtleties of the facial expression and countenance alone'. If you are very, very alert, only then can you see the laughter he called *sita*. If you watch Buddha's face, you will find it there. It is very subtle, very refined. If you are very, very concentrated, only then will you see it, otherwise you will miss it, because it is just in the expression. Not even the lips are moving. In fact, there is no visible thing, it is invisible laughter. That may be the reason Christians think Jesus never laughed: it may have been *sita*. It is said that Sariputra found *sita* on Buddha's face. It was rare. It was very rare because it is one of the most refined things. When your soul reaches to the highest point, only then *sita*. Then it is not something that you do, it is simply there for anybody who is sensitive enough, concentrated enough, to see it.

Second, Sariputra said, *hasita*, 'a smile involving a slight movement of the lips and barely revealing the tips of the teeth'. Third, he called *vihasita*, 'a broad smile accompanied by a modicum of laughter'. Fourth, he called *upahasita*, 'accentuated laughter, louder in volume, associated with movements of the head, shoulders and arms'. Fifth, he called *apahasita*, 'loud laughter that brings tears'. And sixth he called *atihasita*, 'the most boisterous, uproarious laughter, attended by movements of the whole body, doubling over in raucous guffawing, convulsions, hysterics'.

When you concentrate even on a small thing like laughter, it becomes a tremendous, a very big thing—the whole world.

Concentration reveals to you things which are not ordinarily revealed. Ordinarily, you live in a very indifferent mood. You simply go on living as if half asleep—looking, and not looking at all; seeing, and not seeing at all; hearing, and not hearing at all. Concentration brings energy to your eyes. If you look at a thing with a concentrated mind, everything excluded, suddenly, that small thing reveals much that was always there, waiting.

The whole of science is concentration. Watch a scientist working; he is in concentration.

There is an anecdote about Pasteur. He was working. Looking through his microscope, so silent, so unmoving that a visitor had come and waited for long, and he was afraid to disturb him. Something sacred surrounded the scientist. When Pasteur came out of his concentration, he asked the visitor, 'How long have you been waiting? Why didn't you tell me before?'

He said, 'I was going to tell you many times—in fact, I am in a hurry. I have to reach somewhere, and some message has to be delivered to you, but you were in such deep concentration—almost as if praying—that I could not disturb. It was sacred.'

Pasteur said, 'You are right. It is my prayer. Whenever I feel disturbed, and whenever I feel too many worries, and whenever I feel too many thoughts, I simply take my microscope. I look through it—immediately, the old world drops. I am concentrated.'

A scientist's whole work is of concentration, remember this. Science can become the first step towards yoga because concentration is the first inner step of yoga. Each scientist, if he goes on growing and does not get stuck, will become a yogi. He is on the way because he is fulfilling the first condition: concentration.

'*Dharana*, concentration, is confining the mind to the object being meditated upon.'

✍

Dhyan, contemplation, is the uninterrupted flow of the mind of the object.

First, concentration, dropping the crowd of objects and choosing one object. Once you have chosen one object, and you can retain one object in your consciousness, concentration is achieved. Now the second step, uninterrupted flow of consciousness towards the object. As if light is falling from a torch, uninterrupted. Or, have you seen? You pour water from one pot to another pot: the flow will be interrupted; it will not be uninterrupted. You pour oil from one pot to another pot: the flow will be uninterrupted, continuous; the thread will not be broken.

Dhyan, contemplation, means your consciousness falling on the object in continuity, with no break—because each break means you are distracted, you have gone somewhere else. If you can attain the first, the second is not difficult. If you cannot attain the first, the second is impossible. Once you drop objects, you choose one object, then you drop all loopholes in your consciousness, all distractions in your consciousness, you simply pour yourself on one object.

When you look at one object, the object reveals its qualities. A small object can reveal all the qualities of God.

There is a poem of Tennyson. He was going for a morning walk and he came across an old wall, and in the wall there was grass growing, and a small flower had bloomed. He looked at that flower. The morning, he must have been feeling relaxed, happy, energy must have been flowing, the sun was rising . . . Suddenly, the thought occurred to his mind—looking at this small flower—he said, 'If I can understand you, root and all, I will understand the whole universe. Because each small particle is a miniature universe.'

Each small particle carries the whole universe, as each drop carries the whole ocean. If you can understand one drop of ocean, you have understood all oceans; now there is no need to go to understand each drop. One drop will do.

Concentration reveals the qualities of the drop, and the drop becomes the ocean.

Meditation reveals the qualities of consciousness, and the individual consciousness becomes cosmic consciousness. First reveals the object: second reveals the subject. An uninterrupted flow of consciousness towards any object . . . In that uninterrupted flow, in that unfrozen flow, just in that flow . . . you are simply flowing like a river, with no interruption, with no distraction . . . suddenly, you become for the first time aware about the subjectivity that you have been carrying all along, who you are.

In an uninterrupted flow of consciousness, ego disappears. You become the self, egoless self, selfless self. You have also become an ocean.

The second, contemplation, is the way of the artist. The first, concentration, is the way of the scientist. The scientist is concerned with the outside world, not with himself. The artist is concerned with himself, not with the outside world. Then a scientist brings something, he brings it from the objective world. When an artist brings something, he brings it out of himself. A poem: he digs deep in himself. A painting, he digs deep in himself. Don't ask the artist about being objective. He is a subjectivist.

Have you seen Van Gogh's trees? They almost reach to the heavens; they touch the stars. They overreach. Trees like that exist nowhere—except in Van Gogh's paintings. Stars are small, and trees are big. Somebody asked Van Gogh, 'From where do you create these trees? We have never seen such trees.' He said, 'Out of me. Because, to me, trees always seem desires of the earth to meet the sky.' 'Desires of the earth to meet the sky'—then the tree is totally transformed, a metamorphosis has happened. Then the tree is not an object; it has become a subjectivity. As if the artist realizes the tree by becoming a tree himself.

There are many beautiful stories about Zen masters, because Zen masters were great painters and great artists. That is one of the most beautiful things about Zen. No other religion has been so creative, and unless a religion is creative, it is not a total religion—something is missing.

One Zen master used to tell his disciples, 'If you want to paint a bamboo, become a bamboo.' There is no other way. How can you paint a bamboo if you have not felt it from within? . . . if you have not felt yourself as a bamboo standing against the sky, standing against the wind, standing against the rain, standing high with pride in the sun? If you have not heard the noise of the wind passing through the bamboo as the bamboo hears it, if you have not felt the rain falling on the bamboo as the bamboo feels it, how can you paint a bamboo? If you have not heard the sound of the cuckoo as the bamboo hears it, how can you paint a bamboo? Then you paint a bamboo as a photographer. You may be a camera, but you are not an artist.

Camera belongs to the world of science. The camera is scientific. It simply shows the objectivity of the bamboo. But when a master looks at the bamboo, he is not looking from the outside. He drops himself, by and by. His uninterrupted flow of consciousness falls on the bamboo; there happens a meeting, a marriage, a communion, where it is very difficult to say who is bamboo and who is consciousness—everything meets and merges, and boundaries disappear.

The second, *dhyan*, contemplation, is the way of the artist. That's why artists sometimes have glimpses as of the mystics. That's why poetry sometimes says something which prose can never say, and paintings sometimes show something for which there is no other way to show. The artist is reaching even closer to the religious person, to the mystic.

If a poet just remains a poet, he is stuck. He has to flow, he has to move: from concentration to meditation, and from meditation to *samadhi*. One has to go on moving.

Dhyan is uninterrupted flow of the mind to the object. Try it. And it will be good if you choose some object which you love. You can choose your beloved, you can choose your child, you can choose a flower—anything that you love—because in love, it becomes easier to fall uninterruptedly on the object of love. Look in the eyes of your beloved. First forget the whole world; let your beloved be the world. Then look into the eyes and become a continuous flow, uninterrupted, falling into her—oil being poured from one pot into another. No distraction. Suddenly, you will be able to see who you are; you will be able to see your subjectivity for the first time.

But, remember, this is not the end. Object and subject, both are two parts of one whole. Day and night: both are two parts of one whole. Life and death: both are two parts of one whole existence. Object is out, subject is in—you are neither out nor in. This is very difficult to understand because ordinarily it is said, 'Go within.' That is just a temporary phase. One has to go even beyond that. Without and within—both are out. You are that who can go without and who can come within. You are that who can move between these two polarities. You are beyond the polarities. That third state is *samadhi*.

❦

*Samadhi is when the mind becomes one with
the object.*

When the subject disappears in the object, when the object
disappears in the subject, when there is nothing to look at,
and there is no looker-on, when simply the duality is not
there, a tremendously potential silence prevails. You cannot
say what exists, because there is nobody to say. You
cannot make any statement about *samadhi*, because all
statements will fall short. Because whatsoever you can say
either will be scientific or will be poetic. Religion remains
inexpressible, elusive.

So there are two types of religious expressions. Patanjali
tries the scientific terminology. Because religion in itself has
no terminology—the whole cannot be expressed. To express,
it has to be divided. To express, either it has to be put as
an object or as a subject. It has to be divided; to say
anything about it is to divide it. Patanjali chooses the
scientific terminology: Buddha also chooses the scientific
terminology. Lao Tzu, Jesus, they choose the poetic
terminology. But both are terminologies. It depends on the
mind. Patanjali is a scientific mind, very rooted in logic,
analysis. Jesus is a poetic mind; Lao Tzu is a perfect poet,
he chooses the way of poetry. But, remember always, that
both ways fall short. One has to go beyond.

'*Samadhi* is when the mind becomes one with the
object.'

When the mind becomes one with the object, there is
no one who is a knower and there is none who is known.

And unless you come to know this—this knowing
which is beyond the known and the knower—you have
missed your life. You may have been chasing butterflies,

dreams, maybe attaining a little pleasure here and there, but you have missed the ultimate benediction.

A jar of honey having been upset in a housekeeper's room, a number of flies were attracted by its sweetness. Placing their feet in it, they ate greedily. Their feet, however, became so smeared with honey that they could not use their wings nor release themselves and were suffocated. Just as they were expiring, one of them exclaimed, 'Ah, foolish creatures that we are, for the sake of a little pleasure we have destroyed ourselves.'

Remember, this is the possibility for you also. You may get smeared with the earth so much that you cannot use your wings. You may get loaded with your small pleasures so much that you forget all about the ultimate bliss, which was always yours just for the asking. In collecting pebbles and shells on the seashore, you may miss the utterly blissful treasure of your being. Remember this. This is happening. Only rarely does somebody become aware enough not to be caught in this ordinary imprisonment of life.

I am not saying, don't enjoy. The sunshine is beautiful and the flowers also and butterflies also, but don't get lost in them. Enjoy them, nothing is wrong in them, but always remember, the tremendously beautiful is waiting. Relax sometimes in the sunshine, but don't make it a lifestyle. Sometimes relax and play with pebbles on the seashore. Nothing is wrong in it. As a holiday, as a picnic, it can be allowed, but don't make it your very life, then you will miss it. And, remember, wherever you pay your attention, that becomes your reality of life. If you pay your attention to pebbles, they become diamonds—because wherever is your attention, there is your treasure.

I have heard, it happened once:

A railway employee accidentally trapped himself in a refrigerator car. He could neither escape nor attract the attention of anybody to his sad plight, so he resigned himself to a tragic fate. The record of his approaching death was scribbled on the wall of the car in these words, 'I am becoming colder. Still colder now. Nothing to do but wait. These may be my last words.' And they were. When the car was opened, the searchers were astonished to find him dead. There was no physical reason for his death. The temperature of the car was a moderate fifty-six degrees. Only in the mind of the victim did the freezing apparatus work. There was plenty of fresh air: he had not suffocated.

He died of his own wrong attention. He died of his own fears. He died of his own mind. It was a suicide.

Remember, wherever you pay attention, that becomes your reality. And once it becomes a reality, it becomes powerful to attract you and your attention. Then you pay more attention to it: it becomes even more of a reality and, by and by, the unreal that is created by your mind becomes your only reality and the real is completely forgotten.

The real has to be sought. And the only way to reach it is, first, drop too many objects, let there be one object: second, drop all distractions. Let your consciousness fall on that object in an uninterrupted flow. And the third happens by itself. If these two conditions are fulfilled, *Samadhi* happens on its own accord. Suddenly, one day the subject and object both have disappeared: the guest and the host both have disappeared; silence reigns, stillness reigns. In that stillness, you attain to the goal of life.

๕

Patanjali says:

> *The three taken together—dharana, dhyan, and samadhi—constitute sanyama.*

Such a beautiful definition of *sanyama*. Ordinarily, *sanyama* is thought to be a discipline, a controlled state of character. It is not. *Sanyama* is the balance which is attained when subject and object disappear. *Sanyama* is the tranquility when the duality is no more within you and you are not divided and you have become one.

Sometimes it happens naturally also, because if it were not so, Patanjali would not have been able to discover it. Sometimes it happens naturally—it has happened to you also. You cannot find a man to whom there have not been moments of reality. Accidentally, sometimes you fall in tune not knowing the mechanism, how it happens, but sometimes you fall in tune and, suddenly, it is there.

One man wrote me a letter and he said, 'Today, I attained five minutes of reality.' I like the expression, 'five minutes of reality'. 'And how did it happen?' I inquired. He said that he had been ill for a few days. And this is unbelievable, but this is true, that to many people, in illness sometimes tranquility comes—because in illness, your ordinary life is stopped. For a few days he was ill and he was not allowed to move out of bed, so he was relaxing— nothing to do. Relaxed, after four, five days, suddenly, one day it happened. He was just lying down, looking at the ceiling, and it happened—those five minutes of reality.

Everything stopped. Time stopped, space disappeared. There was nothing to look at, and there was nobody to look. Suddenly, there was oneness, as if everything fell in line, became one piece.

To a few people it happens while they are making love. A total orgasm, and after the orgasm, everything silences, everything falls into line . . . one relaxes. The frozenness is gone, one is no longer tense, the storm is gone, and the silence that comes after it . . . and suddenly there is reality.

Sometimes walking in the sun against the wind, enjoying. Sometimes swimming in the river, flowing with the river. Sometimes doing nothing, just relaxing on the sand, looking at the stars, it happens.

But those are just accidents. And because they are accidents, and because they don't fit in your total style of life, you forget them. You don't pay much attention to them. You just shrug your shoulders, and you forget all about them. Otherwise, in everybody's life, sometimes, reality penetrates.

Yoga is a systematic way to reach to that which sometimes happens only accidentally. Yoga makes a science out of all those accidents and coincidences.

The three taken together constitute *sanyama*. The three—concentration, meditation, and *samadhi*—are as if they are the three legs of a three-legged stool, the trinity.

ॐ

By mastering it, the light of higher consciousness.

Those who attain to this trinity of concentration, meditation and *samadhi*, to them happens the light of higher consciousness.

'Climb high, climb far, your goal the sky, your aim the star.' But the journey starts where you are. Step by step, climb high, climb far, your goal the sky, your aim the star. Unless you become as vast as the sky, don't rest; the journey is not yet complete. Unless you reach and become an eternal light, the star, don't become complacent, don't feel contented. Let the divine discontent burn like a fire, so that one day, out of all your efforts the star is born and you become an eternal light.

'*By mastering it, the light of higher consciousness.*' Once you master these three inner steps, the light becomes available to you. And when the inner light is available, you always live in that light: 'At dusk the cock announces dawn. At midnight, the bright sun.' Then even at midnight, there is bright sun available; then even at dusk, the cock announces dawn. When you have the inner light, there is no darkness. Wherever you go, your inner light moves with you—you move in it, you *are* it.

Remember that your mind always tries to make you satisfied wherever you are; the mind says, there is nothing more to life. The mind goes on trying to convince you that you have arrived. The mind does not allow you to become divinely discontent. And it can always find rationalizations. Don't listen to those rationalizations. They are not real reasons: they are tricks of the mind, because the mind does not want to go, to move. Mind is basically lazy. Mind is a sort of entropy: the mind wants to settle, to make your home anywhere but make your home; just settle, don't be a wanderer.

To be a sanyasi means to become a wanderer in consciousness. To be a sanyasi means to become a vagabond—in consciousness—go on searching and wandering. 'Climb high, climb far, your goal the sky, your aim the star.' And don't listen to the mind.

It happened one night:

A policeman was watching a very drunken man vainly trying to fit his house key into a lamp-post.

'It is no use, old chap,' he said. 'There is nobody at home.'

'That is where you are wrong,' replied the fuddled man. 'There is light upstairs.'

The mind is very much fuddled and drunken. It goes on giving reasons. It says, 'What more is there?' Just a few days before, a politician came to me. He said, 'Now what more is there? I was born in a small village to a poor family, and now I have become a Cabinet Minister. What more is there to life?' Cabinet Minister? What more is there to life? he asks, and he is satisfied. 'Born in a village to a poor family, what more can one expect?' While the whole sky was available, he is satisfied in being a Cabinet Minister. Don't get finished that way.

Unless you become a god! Take rest sometimes, by the way, but always remember: it is only a night's rest; by the morning we go.

There are a few people who are satisfied with their worldly achievements. There are a few more who are not satisfied with their worldly achievements but who are satisfied by the promises of the priests. Those, the second category, you call religious. They are also not religious—because religion is not a promise. It has to be attained. Nobody else can promise you; you have to attain it. All promises are consolations and all consolations are dangerous, because they are like opium. They drug you.

It happened:

At an examination of a class in first-aid, a priest was asked (he was also taking the training of first-aid), 'What would you do if you found a man in a fainting condition?'

'I would give him some brandy,' was the answer.

'And if there was no brandy?'

'I would promise him some,' said the priest.

The priest has always been saying that. The priests are the great promisers—they go on issuing promissory notes. They go on saying, 'Don't be worried. Donate, make a church, give money to the poor, make a hospital, this and that, and we promise you.'

Yoga is self-effort. Yoga has no priests. It has only masters who have attained by their own effort—and in their light you have to learn how to attain yourself. Avoid the promises of the priests. They are the most dangerous people on earth, because they don't allow you to become really discontent. They go on consoling you; and if you are consoled before you have attained, you are cheated, you are deceived. Yoga believes in effort, in tremendous effort. One has to become worthy. One has to *earn* God: you have to pay the cost.

Someone once asked the former Prince of Wales, 'What is your idea of civilization?'

'It is a good idea,' replied the prince. 'Somebody ought to start it.'

The yoga is not just an idea, it is a practice, it is *abhyas*, it is a discipline, it is a science of inner transformation. And, remember, nobody can start it for you. You have to start it for yourself. Yoga teaches you to trust yourself; yoga teaches you to become confident of yourself. Yoga teaches you that the journey is alone. A master can indicate the way, but you have to follow it.

ॐ

2. The Mind Is Very Clever

What can I do with a beggar? Whether I give him a rupee or not, he will remain a beggar all the same.

THE BEGGAR IS not the problem. If the beggar was the problem, everybody who passes by would feel the same. If the beggar was the problem, beggars would have disappeared long ago. The problem is within you: your heart feels it. Try to understand it.

The mind interferes immediately whenever the heart feels love, the mind immediately interferes. The mind says, 'Whether you give him something or not, he will remain a beggar all the same.' Whether he remains a beggar or not is not your responsibility, but if your heart feels to do something, do it. Don't try to avoid. The mind is trying to avoid the situation. The mind says, 'What is going to happen? He will remain a beggar, so there is no need to do anything.' You have missed an opportunity where your love could have flown.

If the beggar has decided to be a beggar, you cannot do

anything. You may give him: he may throw it. That is for him to decide.

The mind is very clever.

ॐ

Then the question, it says:

> *Why are there beggars at all?*

Because there is no love in the human heart. But again, the mind interferes:

> *Have not the rich taken away from the poor?*
> *Should not the poor take back what the rich*
> *have stolen from him?*

Now you are forgetting the beggar and the heartache that you felt. Now the whole thing is becoming political, economical. Now the problem is no more of the heart: it is of the mind. And mind has created the beggar. It is the cunningness, the calculativeness of the mind that has created the beggar. There are cunning people, very calculative: they have become rich. There are innocent people, not so calculative, not so cunning: they have become poor.

You can change society—in Soviet Russia they have changed. That makes no difference. Now the old categories have disappeared—the poor and the rich—but the ruler and the ruled, a new category has come up. Now the cunning are the rulers and the innocent are the ruled. Before, the innocent used to be poor, and the cunning used to be rich. What can you do?

Unless the division between mind and heart is dissolved, unless humanity starts living through the heart and not through the mind, the classes are going to remain. The names will change, and misery is going to continue.

The question is very relevant, very meaningful, significant. *What can I do with a beggar?* Beggar is not the question. The question is you and your heart. Do something, whatsoever you can do, and don't try to throw the responsibility on the rich. Don't try to throw the responsibility on history. Don't try to throw the responsibility on the economic structure. Because that is secondary: if humanity remains cunning and calculative, it is going to be repeated again and again and again.

What can you do for it? You are a small part of the total. Whatsoever you do will not change the situation—but it will change you. It may not change the beggar if you give something to him, but the very gesture, that you shared whatsoever you could, will change you. And that is important. And if this goes on—the revolution of the heart—people who feel, people who look at another human being as an end in itself, if this goes on increasing, one day, the poor people will disappear, poverty will disappear—and it will not be replaced by a new category of exploitation.

Up to now all the revolutions have failed, because the revolutionaries have not been able to see the basic cause why there is poverty. They are looking only at superficial causes. Immediately, they say, 'Some people have exploited him, that's why their possibility. This is the cause; that's why there is poverty.'

But why were some people able to exploit? Why could they not see? Why could they not see that they are gaining nothing and this man is losing all? They may accumulate wealth, but they are killing life all around. Their wealth is nothing but blood. Why can they not see it? The cunning mind has created explanations there also.

The cunning mind says, 'People are poor because of their *karma*. In the past lives, they have done something wrong, that's why they are suffering. I am rich because I have done good deeds, so I am enjoying the fruit.' This is also mind. And Marx sitting in the British Museum is also a mind: and thinking about what is the basic cause of poverty comes to feel that there are people who exploit. But these people will be there always. Unless cunningness disappears completely; it is not a question of changing the structure of society. It is a question of changing the whole structure of human personality.

What can you do? You can change, you can throw out the rich people—they will come back from the back door. They were cunning. In fact, those who are throwing, they are also very cunning; otherwise they cannot throw. The rich people may not be able to come from the back door, but the people who call themselves revolutionaries, communists, socialists—they will sit on the throne and then they will start exploiting. And they will exploit more dangerously because they have proved themselves more cunning than the rich. By throwing out the rich, they have proved one thing absolutely: that they are more cunning than the rich. Society will be in the hands of more cunning people.

And, remember, if someday some other revolutionaries are born—which are bound to be, because again people will start feeling the exploitation is there, now it has taken a new form—again there will be a revolution. But who will throw the past revolutionaries? Now more cunning people will be needed.

Whenever you are going to defeat a certain system, and you use the same means as the system has used for itself, just names will change, flags will change, society will remain the same.

Enough of this befooling. The beggar is not the question: the question is you. Don't be cunning, don't be clever. Don't try to say that this is his *karma*—you don't know anything about *karma*. That is just a hypothesis to explain certain things which are unexplained, to explain certain things which cause heartache. Once you accept the hypothesis, you are relieved of the burden. Then you can remain rich and the poor can remain poor and there is no problem. The hypothesis functions as a buffer.

That's why in India poverty has remained so ingrained and people have become so insensitive towards it. They have a certain theory which helps them. Just as you move in a car and the car has shock absorbers, the roughness of the road is not felt, the shock absorbers go on absorbing; this hypothesis of *karma* is a great shock absorber. You come constantly against poverty, but there is a shock absorber: the theory of *karma*. What can you do? It has nothing to do with yourself. You are enjoying your riches because of your virtues—good deeds done in the past. And this man is suffering from his bad deeds.

There is in India a certain sect of Jainism, Tera-Panth. They are the extremist believers of this theory. They say, 'Don't interfere, because he is suffering his past *karma*s. Don't interfere. Don't give him anything, because that will be an interference, and he could have suffered in a short time—you will be delaying the process. He will have to suffer.'

For example, a poor man, you can give him enough to live at ease for a few years, but again the suffering will start. You can give him enough to live at ease in this life, but again in the next life the suffering will start. Where you stopped it, exactly from there the suffering will start again. So those who believe in the Tera-Panth, they go on saying: don't interfere. Even if somebody is dying by the side of the road, you simply go on indifferent on your path. They say this is compassion; interfering, you delay the process.

What a great shock absorber!

In India, people have become absolutely insensitive. A cunning theory protects them.

In the West, they have found a new hypothesis: that it is because the rich have exploited—so destroy the rich. Just look at it. Looking at a poor man, love starts rising in your heart. You immediately say, this poor man is poor because of the rich. You have turned love into hate; now hate arises towards the rich man. What game are you playing? Now you say, 'Destroy the rich! Take everything back from them. They are the criminals.' Now the beggar is forgotten; the heart is full of love no more. On the contrary, it is full of hate . . . and hate has created the society in which beggars exist. Now again hate is functioning in you. You will create a society in which categories may change, names may change, but there will be the ruled and the rulers, the exploited and the exploiters, the oppressors and the oppressed. It will not make much difference; it will remain the same. There will be masters and there will be slaves.

The only revolution possible is the revolution of the heart. When you see a beggar, remain sensitive. Don't allow any shock absorber to come between you and the beggar. Remain sensitive. It is difficult because you will start crying. It is difficult because it will be very, very uncomfortable. Share whatsoever you can share. And don't be worried whether he will remain a beggar or not—you did whatsoever you could. And this will change you. This will give you a new being, closer to the heart and farther away from the mind. This is your inner transformation; and this is the only way.

If individuals go on changing in this way, there may some time arise a society where people are so sensitive that they cannot exploit, where people have become so alert and aware that they cannot oppress, where people have become so loving that just to think of poverty, of slavery, is impossible.

Do something out of the heart, and don't fall a victim of theories.

ॐ

The questioner goes on:

> You have said we must move to the opposite pole; we must choose both science and religion, rationality and irrationality, west and east, technology and spirituality. Can I choose both politics and meditation? Can I choose to change the world and to change myself at the same time? Can I be a revolutionary and a sanyasi at once?

Yes, I have said again and again that one has to accept the polarities. But meditation is not a pole. Meditation is the acceptance of the polarities, and through that acceptance, one transcends beyond the polarities. So there is no opposite to meditation. Try to understand.

You are sitting in your room full of darkness. Is darkness the opposite of light, or just the absence of light? If it is opposite to light, it has its own existence. Does darkness have its own existence? Is it real in its own way, or is it just the absence of light? If it has a reality of its own, when you light a candle, it will resist. It will try to put the candle off. It will fight for its own existence; it will resist. But it gives no resistance. It never fights, it can never put a small candle . . . Vast darkness and a small candle, but the candle cannot be defeated by that vast darkness. The darkness may have ruled in that house for centuries, but you bring a small candle, the darkness cannot say, 'I am centuries old and I will give a good fight.' It simply disappears.

Darkness has no positive reality, it is simply the absence of light, so when you bring light, it disappears. When you put the light off, it appears. In fact, it never goes out and never comes in, because it cannot go out and cannot come in. Darkness is nothing but the absence of light. Light present, it is not there; light absent, it is there. It is absence.

Meditation is the inner light. It has no opposite, only absence.

The whole life is an absence of meditation, as you live it, the worldly life—the life of power, prestige, ego, ambition, greed. And that is what politics is.

Politics is a very big word. It does not include only the so-called politicians, it includes all the worldly people, because whosoever is ambitious is a politician, and whosoever is struggling to reach somewhere is a politician. Wherever there is competition, there is politics. Thirty students studying in the same class and calling themselves class fellows—they are class enemies, because they are all competing, not fellows. They are all trying to overtake the other. They are all trying to get the gold medal, to come first. The ambition is there: they are already politicians.

Wherever there is competition and struggle, there is politics. So the whole ordinary life is politics-oriented.

Meditation is like light: when meditation comes, politics disappears. So you cannot be meditative and political. That is impossible: you are asking for the impossible. Meditation is not one pole: it is the absence of all conflict, all ambition, all ego trips.

Let me tell you a very famous Sufi story. It happened:

A Sufi said, 'None can understand man until he realizes the connection between greed, obligingness, and impossibility.'

'This,' said his disciple, 'is a conundrum which I cannot understand.'

The Sufi said, 'Never look for understanding through conundrums when you can attain it through experience directly.'

He took the disciple to a shop in the nearby market where robes were sold. 'Show me your very best robe,' said the Sufi to the shopkeeper, 'for I am in a mood to spend excessively.'

A most beautiful garment was produced, and an extremely high price was asked for it. 'It is very much the kind of thing I would like,' said the Sufi, 'but I would like some sequins around the collar and a touch of fur trimming.'

'Nothing easier,' said the seller of the robes, 'for I have just such a garment in the workroom of my shop.' He disappeared for a few moments and then returned having added the fur and the sequins to the selfsame garment.

'And how much is this one?' asked the Sufi.

'Twenty times the price of the first one,' said the shopkeeper.

'Excellent,' said the Sufi. 'I shall take both of them.'

Now, the impossibility, because it is the selfsame garment. The Sufi was showing that greed has a certain impossibility in it; impossibility is intrinsic to greed.

Now don't be too greedy, because this is the greatest greed there is to ask to be a politician and a meditator together, simultaneously. That is the greatest greed possible. You are asking to be ambitious and non-tense. You are asking to fight, to be violent, to be greedy, and yet peaceful and relaxed. If it were possible, there would have been no need for *sanyas*, then there would have been no need for meditation.

You cannot have both. Once you start meditating, politics starts disappearing. With politics, all the effects of it also disappear. The tense state, the worry, the anxiety, the anguish, the violence, the greed—they all disappear. They are by-products of a political mind.

You will have to decide: either you can be a politician or you can be a meditator. You cannot be both, because when meditation comes, the darkness disappears. *This* world, your world, is an absence of meditation. And when meditation comes, this world simply disappears like darkness.

That's why Patanjali, Shankara, and others who have known, go on saying that this world is illusory, not real. Illusory like darkness, appears to be real, when it is there, but once you bring light in, suddenly you become aware it was not real, it was unreal. Just look into darkness. How real it is. How real it looks. It is there surrounding you from everywhere. Not only that—you are feeling afraid. The unreal creating fear. It can kill you, and it is not there!

Bring light. Keep somebody by the door to see whether or not he comes to see the darkness going out. Nobody ever sees darkness going out; nobody ever sees darkness coming in. It appears to be and it is not.

The so-called world of desire and ambition, politics, only appears to be and it is not. Once you meditate, you start laughing about the whole nonsense, the whole nightmare that has disappeared.

But please don't try to do this impossible thing. If you try, you will be in much conflict; you will become a split personality. 'Can I choose both politics and meditation? Can I choose to change the world and to change myself at the same time?' Not possible.

In fact, you are the world. When you change yourself, you have started to change the world—and there is no other way. If you start changing others, you will not be able to change yourself, and one who is not able to change himself, cannot change anybody. He can only go on believing that he is doing great work, as your politicians go on believing.

Your so-called revolutionaries are all ill people, tense people, mad people—insane—but their insanity is such that if they are left to themselves, they will go completely mad, so they put their insanity in some occupation. Either they start changing society, reforming society, doing this and that . . . changing the whole world. And their madness is such they cannot see the stupidity of it: you have not changed yourself—how can you change anybody else?

Start closer at home. First change yourself, first bring the light within yourself, then you will be capable . . . In fact, to say then there will be any capacity to change others is not right. In fact, once you change yourself, you become a source of infinite energy, and that energy changes others on its own accord. Not that you go on and work hard and become a martyr in changing people; no, nothing of that sort. You simply remain in yourself, but the very energy, the purity of it, the innocence of it, the fragrance of it, goes on spreading in ripples. It reaches to all the shores of the world. Without any effort on your side, an effortless revolution starts. And the revolution is beautiful when it is effortless. When it is with effort, it is violent, then you are forcing your ideas on somebody else.

Stalin killed millions of people because he was a revolutionary. He wanted to change society, and whosoever was obstructing in any way, had to be killed and removed from the way. Sometimes it happens that those who are trying to help you, they start helping even *against* you. They don't bother whether you want to be changed or not; they have an idea to change you. They will change you in spite of you. They won't listen to you. This type of revolution is going to be violent, bloody.

And a revolution cannot be violent, cannot be bloody, because a revolution has to be a revolution of love and heart. A real revolutionary never goes anywhere to change anybody. He remains rooted in himself; and people who want to be changed, they come to him. They travel from faraway lands. They come to him. The fragrance reaches them. In subtle ways, in unknown ways, whosoever wants to change himself comes and seeks a revolutionary. The real revolutionary remains in himself, available. Like a pool of cool water. Whosoever is thirsty will seek. The pool is not going to search for you; the pool is not going to run after you. And the pool is not going to drown you because you are thirsty—that if you don't listen, then the pool will drown you.

Stalin killed so many people. Revolutionaries have been as violent as reactionaries—and sometimes even more so.

Please don't try to do the impossible. Just change yourself. In fact, that too is such an impossibility, that if you can change yourself in this life, you can feel grateful. You can say, 'Enough, more than enough has happened.'

Don't be worried about others. They are also beings, they have consciousness, they have souls. If they want to change, nobody is hindering the path. Remain a pool of cool water. If they are thirsty, they will come. Just your coolness will be the invitation, your purity of water will be the attraction.

'Can I be a revolutionary and a sanyasi at once?' No. If you are a sanyasi, you are a revolution, not a revolutionary. You need not be a revolutionary if you are a sanyasi, you are a revolution. Try to understand what I am saying. Then you don't go to change people, don't go to create any revolution anywhere. You don't plan it—you *live* it. Your very style of life is revolution. Wherever you will look, wherever you will touch, there will be revolution. Revolution will become just like breathing—spontaneous.

Another Sufi story I would like to tell you:

A well-known Sufi was asked, 'What is invisibility?' and he said, 'I shall answer that when an opportunity for a demonstration occurs.' Sufis don't talk much. They create situations. They don't say much; they show through situations. So the Sufi said, 'Whenever an opportunity occurs, I will give you a demonstration.'

Sometime later, that man and the one who had asked him the question were stopped by a band of soldiers, and the soldiers said, 'We have orders to take all dervishes into custody, for the king of this country says that they will not obey his commands and that they say things which are not welcome to the tranquility of thought of the populace. So we are going to imprison all the Sufis.'

Whenever there is a really religious person, a revolution, the politicians become very much afraid, because his very presence *maddens* them. His very presence is enough to create chaos. His very presence is enough to create disorder, a death to the old society. His very presence is enough to create a new world. He becomes a vehicle. Absent, completely absent as far as his ego is concerned, he becomes a vehicle of the divine. The rulers, the cunning people, have always been afraid of religious people because there cannot be more danger than a religious person. They are not afraid of revolutionaries, because their strategies are the same. They are not afraid of revolutionaries, because they use the same language, their terminology is the same. They are the same people; they are not different people.

Just go to New Delhi and watch the politicians. All the politicians who are in power and all the politicians who are not in power—they are all the same people. Those who are in power seem to be reactionaries because they have attained power; now they want to protect it. Now they want to keep it in their hands, so they seem to be the establishment. Those who are not in power—they talk about revolution because they want to throw out those who are in power. Once they are in power, they will become the reactionaries, and the people who were in power, who were thrown out of power, they will become the revolutionaries.

A successful revolutionary is a dead revolutionary, and a ruler thrown out of his power becomes a revolutionary. And they go on deceiving the people. Whether you choose those who are in power, or those who are not in power, you are not choosing different people. You are choosing the same people. They have different labels, but there is not a bit of difference.

A religious person is a real danger. His very being is dangerous, because he brings through him new worlds.

The soldiers surrounded the Sufi and his disciple, and they said they are in search of Sufis, all Sufis have to be imprisoned, because the king has commanded so, saying that they say things which are not welcome and they create such thought patterns which are not good for the tranquility of the populace.

And the Sufi said, 'And so you should . . .' And the Sufi said to the soldiers, 'And so you should . . . for you must do your duty.'

'But are you not Sufis?' asked the soldiers.

'Test us,' said the Sufi.

The officer took out a Sufi book. 'What is this?' he asked.

The Sufi looked at the title page and said, 'Something which I will burn in front of you since you have not already done so.' He set light to the book, and the soldiers rode away satisfied.

The Sufi's companion asked, 'What was the purpose of that action?'

'To make us invisible,' said the Sufi, 'for to the man of the world, visibility means that you are looking like something or someone he expects you to resemble. If you look different, your true nature becomes invisible to him.'

A religious man lives a life of revolution, but invisible. Because to become visible is to become gross, to become visible is to come to the lowest rung of the ladder. A religious person, a sanyasi, creates a revolution in himself and remains invisible. And that invisible source of energy goes on doing miracles.

Please, if you are a sanyasi, there is no need to be a revolutionary; you are already a revolution. And I say a revolution because a revolutionary is already dead, a revolutionary already has fixed ideas—a revolutionary already has a mind. I say *revolution*; it is a process. A sanyasi has no fixed ideas: he lives moment to moment. He responds to the reality of the moment—not out of fixed ideas.

Just watch. Talk to a communist and you will see that he is not listening. He may be nodding his head, but he is not listening. Talk to a Catholic, he is not listening. Talk to a Hindu, he is not listening. While you are talking, he is preparing his answer—from his old, past, fixed ideas. You can even see on the face, there is no response, a dullness and deadness. Talk to a child, he listens, he listens attentively. If he listens at all, he listens attentively. If he does not listen, he is absolutely absent, but he is total. Talk to a child, and you will see the response, pure and fresh.

A sanyasi is like a child, innocent. He does not live out of his ideas: he is not a slave to any ideology. He lives out of consciousness, he lives out of awareness. He acts here-now! He has no yesterdays and he has no tomorrows, only today.

When Jesus was crucified, one thief who was at his side,

said to him, 'We are criminals. We are crucified, that's okay—we can understand. You look innocent. But I am happy just to be crucified with you. I am tremendously happy. I have never done anything good.'

He had completely forgotten something. When Jesus was born, Jesus' parents were escaping from the country because the king had ordered a mass murder of all the children born in a certain period. The king had come to know from his wise men that a revolution is going to be born and there is going to be danger. It is better to prevent it beforehand, take precaution. So he had ordered a mass murder. Jesus' parents were escaping.

One night they were surrounded by a few thieves and robbers—this thief was one of that group—and they were going to rob and kill them. But this thief looked at the child Jesus, and he was so beautiful, and he was so innocent, so pure, as if purity itself . . . and a certain glow was surrounding him. And he stopped the other thieves, and he said, 'Let them go. Just look at the child.' And they all looked at the child: and they all were in a certain hypnosis. They couldn't do what they wanted to do . . . and they left them.

This was the thief who had saved Jesus, but he was not aware that this is the same man. He said to Jesus, 'I don't know what I have done, because I have never done a good deed. You cannot find a greater criminal than me. My whole life was that of sin—robbery, murder, and everything you can imagine. But I am happy. I am thankful to God that I am dying by the side of such an innocent man.'

Jesus said, 'Just because of this gratefulness, you will be in the kingdom of God with me *today*.'

Now, after that statement, Christian theologians have been

continuously discussing what he meant by 'today'. He simply meant now. Because a religious man has no yesterdays, no tomorrows, only today. This moment is all. When he said to the thief, 'Today you will be with me in the kingdom of God,' in fact, he was saying, 'Look! You are already. This very moment, by your gratefulness, by your recognition of purity and innocence—by your repentance—the past has disappeared. We are in the kingdom of God.'

A religious man lives not out of past ideologies, ideas, fixed concepts, philosophies. He lives in this moment. Out of his consciousness, he responds. He is always fresh like a fresh spring, always fresh, uncorrupted by the past.

So, if you are a sanyasi, you are a revolution. A revolution is greater than all the revolutionaries. Revolutionaries are those who have stopped somewhere; the river has become frozen, it flows no more. A sanyasi is always flowing; the river never stops—it goes on and on, flowing and flowing. A sanyasi is a flow.

ॐ

Osho, are you a yogi, or a bhakta. Or a Gyani.
Or a Tantrika?

Nothing of the nonsense.

Don't try to label me; don't try to categorize. The mind would like to put me in a pigeon-hole so you can say this man is this, and you can be finished with me. It is not going to be that easy. I will not allow. I will remain like mercury: the more you will try to grasp me, the more I will become elusive. Either I am all or I am nothing—only these two categories can be allowed, and all other categories in between are not allowed, because they are not going to say the truth. And the day you will realize me, either as all or as nothing, will be a day of great realization to you.

Let me tell you a story I was just reading yesterday. In his story, *The Country of the Blind*, H.G. Wells tells how a traveller came to a strange valley, set off from the rest of the world by precipitous walls, in which all the people were blind—the valley of the blind. A traveller reached there. He lived for a while in this strange place, but was considered queer by the natives. Their experts said, 'His brain is affected by these queer things called the eyes, which keep it in a constant state of irritation and distraction.' And they concluded that he would never be normal until his eyes were removed. 'A surgery is needed, and it is urgent,' the experts said.

They were all blind. They could not conceive how a man can have eyes. Something abnormal, something which has to be removed to make this man normal.

The traveller fell in love with a sightless maiden, who pleaded with him to have his eyes removed so that they might live together in happiness.

'Because,' the woman said, 'if you don't remove your eyes, my community is not going to accept you. You are abnormal; you are so strange. Some misfortune has befallen you. One has never heard about these eyes. And you can ask people; nobody has ever seen. Because of these two eyes, you will remain a stranger in my community and they won't allow me to live with you. And I am also a little afraid to live with you. You are so different, so alien.'

She persuaded him to please let his eyes be removed so that they might live together in happiness. And he was just on the verge of accepting the offer, because he had fallen in love with this blind girl—because of that love and attachment, he was ready even to lose his eyes—but one day when he was just on the verge of deciding, one morning he saw the sun rise on the rocks, and the meadows beautiful with white flowers . . . no longer could he be content in the valley of darkness. He climbed back to the land where men walk in the light.

Buddha, Jesus, Krishna, Zarathustra, they are men with eyes in the valley of the blind. Call them what you like—yogis, buddhas, *jinas*, Christs, *bhaktas*. Call them what you like, but all your categories simply say one thing: that they are different than you, that they have a certain quality of vision, that they have eyes, that they can see something which you cannot see.

And you feel offended: hence, in the beginning you oppose them, even when you start following them. Because their visions create a great desire in you—in spite of your opposition. Deep down in you your own nature goes on saying that these eyes are possible to you also. On the surface, you go on denying; deep down, an undercurrent goes on saying to you that maybe you are not right. Maybe these eyes are normal, and you are abnormal. Maybe you are in a majority, but that doesn't make it a truth.

These people are to be remembered as people with eyes amongst the valley of the blind.

I am here amongst you. I know your difficulty, because that which I can see, you cannot see, that which I can feel, you cannot feel, that which I can touch, you cannot touch. I know even if you become convinced with me, deep down, somewhere a doubt goes on lingering. A doubt—who knows?—this man may be imagining. Who knows?—this man may be just deceiving. Who knows? Because until it becomes an experience in you, how can you trust?

You would like to categorize me. That will give you at least a name, a label, and you will feel comfortable. Then you will start feeling that you know me if you can categorize, that he is a yogi. Then you don't feel so uncomfortable. At least you feel that you know. By naming, people feel that they know. That's an obsession.

A child asks you, 'What flower is this?' He is uncomfortable with the flower because with the flower he can feel the unknown—something which makes him aware of his ignorance. Then you tell him, 'This is a rose.' He is happy. He repeats the name, 'This is a rose, this is a rose.' He goes to other children and he is very happy and says, 'Look, this is a rose.' What has he learned? Just a name. But now he is at ease; now he is no longer ignorant. At least he cannot feel his ignorance now—now he is knowledgeable. Now there is no unknown there; the rose is no longer an unknown entering into the world of the known; it has become part of the known. Just by giving it a name, just by calling it a 'rose,' what have you done?

Whenever you meet somebody strange, you immediately ask, 'What is your name?' Why? Why can't you live with the nameless? And everybody is nameless. Nobody comes with a name; everybody is born without a name. Immediately the child is born, and the family is already thinking what name to give. Why are you in such a hurry? Because again an unknown stranger has entered into your world. You have to label it. Immediately, once you label it, you are satisfied: you know this is Ram, Rahim—something.

All names are absurd. And this small boy has no name.

He is as nameless as God. But a name has to be given; a certain obsession in the human mind and a certain idea that once you name a thing, you have known it. Then you are finished with it.

People come to me. They ask me, 'Who are you? Hindu, Jaina, Mohammedan, Christian? Who are you?' If they can categorize, that I am a Hindu, they will feel satisfied—they know me. Now the word 'Hindu' will give them a false feeling of knowing.

You ask me, 'Who are you? A *bhakta*, a yogi, a *gyani*, a *tantrika*?' If you can find a name, you will be at ease. Then you can relax, then there is no problem.

But will you be able to know me by giving me a name? In fact, if you really want to know me, please don't bring a name in between me and you. Drop all categories. Just look direct. Let your eyes be open and clean of all dust. Look at me without knowledge. Look at me with a simple, innocent look, with no ideas, no prejudices behind, and you will be able to see through and through. I will become transparent to you. That's the only way to know me, that's the only way to know the reality.

Look at the rose and forget the word 'rose'. Look at the tree and forget the word 'tree'. Look at the greenery and forget the word 'green'. And immediately, you will become aware of a strange presence surrounding you that is God.

God labelled becomes the world; world unlabelled again, becomes God. God conditioned in your mind becomes the world; the world unconditioned, again unstructured, again unknown, becomes God.

ॐ

Look at me without any words.

*How to surrender if I am afraid of myself? And
my heart is paining. Where is the door of love?*

There is no 'how' to surrender. If you understand the
stupidity of the ego, the foolishness of the ego, if you
understand the misery of the ego, you drop it. There is no
'how'. Just the very misery of it: you look into it and you
find it absolutely miserable, a hell—you drop it. You go on
clinging to it because, still, you are cherishing a dream
through it. You have not understood the misery of it; you
are still hoping that there may be some treasure in it.

Watch deep in yourself. Don't ask how to drop it; just
see how you are clinging to it. The clinging is the problem.
If you don't cling to it, it drops on its own accord. And if
you ask me how to drop it and you have not seen that you
are clinging to it, I can give you a technique; you will cling
to your ego and you will start clinging to the technique
also. Because you have not understood the process of
clinging.

I have heard an anecdote. There was a professor of
philosophy, a very absent-minded man, as philosophers
are, almost always tend to be—absent-minded. Not that
they have attained to no-mind because their minds are
occupied so much that they are absent from everywhere
else. They are only in the heads. He mislaid everything.
One day he returned home without his umbrella, and his
wife tried to get some indication from him of where to
look for it.

'Tell me,' she said, 'precisely, when did you first miss
it?'

Now this is a wrong question to ask a man who is absent-minded. 'Precisely, where did you miss it?' or 'Where did you, for this first time, become aware that you are missing it?' This is a wrong question, because the person who has forgotten the umbrella, he must have forgotten by now precisely when.

'Tell me,' she said, 'precisely, when did you first miss it?'

'My dear,' he replied, 'it was when I put my hand up to let it down after a short shower. Then I realized it is not there.'

You are clinging, and you ask how to drop it. And the clinging mind will start clinging to the technique. Please, don't ask the 'how'; rather, search within yourself—why you are clinging. What has it given to you up to now, your ego? Has it given anything except promises? Has it fulfilled any promise ever? Are you going to be deceived by it forever and forever? Have you not been deceived by it enough by now? Are you still not contented? Are you still not aware that it is not leading you anywhere, just as in a whirlpool, you go round and round and round, hoping the same old dreams? Every time you get frustrated, you don't see that from the very beginning, the promise was false. The moment you get frustrated, again you start dreaming a new hope and the ego goes on promising you.

The ego is impotent. It can only promise; it can never deliver. Look into it. And on the way, between promise and no delivery, in between the two much suffering, much frustration, much misery.

The hell that you have heard about is not part of geography, it is not underneath earth. It is just underneath your ego. When you become aware of the misery of the ego, you don't cling, that's all. I don't say you drop, you don't cling. Immediately, surrender happens. Surrender is the absence of the ego.

But you never ask, 'Why do I cling to the ego?' You ask, 'How to surrender?' You ask a wrong question.

And, then, there are a thousand and one things which people go on saying to you. Then you cling to them. You are clinging to so many so-called methods, techniques, philosophies, religions, churches. Just to drop one ego you have created three hundred religions in the world. Just to drop one small ego. And millions of techniques and methods, and thousands and thousands of books are being written continuously how to drop it. And the more you read, the more you become knowledgeable, the less is the possibility to drop it—because now you have more to cling to. Now your ego is almost so decorated . . .

I was reading the autobiography of a very well-known novelist. Towards the end of his life, he used to say to everybody and complain, 'I wasted my life. I never wanted to be a novelist—never.' Somebody asked him, 'Then why didn't you stop? Because for at least twenty years I have been listening to you, and I know people who say that they have been listening to your complaint even longer. Why didn't you stop?' He said, 'How could I? Because by the time I realized that this is not my vocation, I had already become famous. By the time I realized that this is not my vocation, I was already a famous novelist.'

You cannot drop the ego if you go on decorating it. Your knowledge decorates it. Your going to the church decorates it—you become religious. Your reading the Bible every day, or the Gita, decorates it. You can look at others with the look, 'holier than you'. You can look with condemnation in your eyes, that the whole world is going to hell—except you.

You go on trying to become humble, to become simple, but deep down in your simplicity sits the ego, enthroned.

And you go on finding rationalizations for it. All rationalizations are decorations.

In India, there was one man, he died a few years before, Nizam of Hyderabad. He was the richest man in the whole world. Your Rockefellers and Fords are nothing. He was the richest man in the world. In fact, nobody knows how much he had exactly, because all his wealth consisted of millions of diamonds. In seven big halls the diamonds were put; the halls were completely full. Even he was not aware of the exact number. But the man was a great miser—you cannot believe. You will simply say that I am lying. He was such a miser that when guests will come and they will leave their half cigarettes on the ashtray, he will collect them and smoke them. You will not believe me, but this is the truth.

When he became Nizam of Hyderabad, he was enthroned; he used the same cap for forty years. That was the dirtiest cap in the world. It was never washed because he was afraid it may be destroyed. He lived the life of a very poor man, but he used to say to his people, 'I am a simple man. Maybe I am the richest man, but I live the life of a poor man.' But he was not poor. He was simply a miser! He used to say that because he is not attached to things and worldly exhibitions, that's why he lives such a simple life. He used to think himself a sadhu, a fakir. He was not. He was the most miserly man ever; the richest and the most miserly. But for his miserliness, he will find rationalizations.

He was so afraid, so superstitious . . . He used to pray and he used to pretend that he is a great prayer. But he was not; he was simply afraid. In the night he used to sleep with a peculiar thing. He had a big pot which he used to fill with salt, and in the pot he will put one of his feet— the whole night. Because Mohammedans have an idea that if your feet are touching salt, ghosts cannot trouble you.

How can this man pray? One who is so afraid of ghosts, how can he love God? Because one who loves God, his fear disappears. But he deceived many people. Or, even if he didn't deceive many people, he deceived himself at least.

Remember, always start from the beginning. Look where you are clinging and why you are clinging. Don't ask for the 'how' to surrender. Just watch and find out why you are clinging to the ego, why you are stubborn.

If you still feel that the ego is going to deliver some heaven for you, then wait—no need to surrender. If you feel that all promises are false and the ego is a deceiver, what is the need to ask how to surrender? Don't cling. In fact, once you know that this is fire, you drop it. It is not a question of not clinging. You simply drop it. When you come to know that your house is on fire, you don't ask anybody how to get out.

Once it happened, I was staying in a house, and just in front of the house, a house caught fire. It was a three-storeyed house, and one fat man, who used to live on the third storey, was trying to jump from the window. The whole crowd was saying, 'Don't jump! We are bringing a ladder!' But who listens when the house is on fire? He jumped. He could not even wait for the ladder. And there was no danger yet because the fire was just on the first storey. To reach to the third, it would have taken time, and the ladder was being brought, and the whole crowd was shouting at him, 'Wait!!' But he couldn't listen. He jumped and broke his leg.

Later on, I went to see him and I asked, 'You did a miracle. You didn't ask how to jump. Have you ever jumped from a three-storey building before?'

He said, 'Never.'

'Have you ever practised?'

He said, 'Never.'

'Any rehearsal?'

He said, 'What are you talking about! This is for the first time!'

'Did you consult any book? You asked for a teacher? You inquired of somebody?'

He said, 'What are you talking about? I could not even wait for my wife to come, my children to come, and I couldn't even understand why the people were shouting so much. Only later on, when I was lying on the ground, then I could understand that they were bringing a ladder.'

When the house is on fire, you jump out of it. You don't ask the 'How?' And I tell you, your house is on fire. Immediately, you ask how to jump out of it. No, you have not understood the point. Still you don't feel that your house is on fire, I say, so my saying creates in you an idea, 'How to jump out of it?' If really you understand that your house is on fire, even if I shout, 'I am bringing a ladder!

Wait!' you are not going to wait. You will jump. You may break your legs.

But, at ease, comfortably, conveniently, you ask, 'How to surrender?' There is no 'how'. Just look at the misery that the ego creates. If you can feel it, you will come out of it.

'And my heart is paining.' It is bound to be so. With the ego, there is going to be much pain.

And you ask, 'Where is the door of love?' Come out of the ego. There is the door of love. Come out of the ego, and there is the door of the heart. The ego prevents you from love, the ego prevents you from meditation, the ego prevents you from prayer, the ego prevents you from God, but still you go on listening to it. Then it is up to you.

This is your choice, remember. Nobody has forced you to listen to the ego. It is your choice. If you choose, it is okay. Then don't ask the 'How?' If you don't choose it, there is no need to ask the 'How?'

❦

Why, when I try to listen to your lectures with
total attention, can I afterwards not remember
what you have said?

There is no need. If you have listened to me with total attention, there is no need to remember what I have said. It becomes part of you. You eat something, do you remember what you have eaten? What is the use? It becomes part of you—it becomes your blood; it becomes your bones. It becomes *you*. Once you eat something, you forget about it. You digest it, not that you remember it.

If you listen totally, I am converting into your blood,

I am converting into your bones, I am converting into your being. You are digesting me.

There is no need. Whenever there will be a situation, you will respond; and in that response, all that you have heard and listened to in totality will be there—but not as remembered . . . but as lived. And this difference has to be remembered.

Whatsoever I am trying here is not to make you more knowledgeable, to give you some information. That is not the purpose of my talking or my being here with you. My whole purpose is to give you more being, not more knowledge. So remain with me, listen totally; there is no need to remember afterwards. It becomes part of you. Whenever there will be a *need*, it will arise. And it will not arise as a memory; it will arise as your living response.

Otherwise, there is always a fear it can become your memory. Then, you are not changed; only your memory tank becomes bigger and bigger and bigger. Your computer becomes more informed. And whenever there will be a real situation, you will forget: then you will act out of your consciousness, not out of your memory. Then you will forget me. When there will be no real situation and you will be arguing with people and discussing, you will remember.

Watch. If what I say becomes just a memory in you, it will be good for discussion, argument, debate—showing your knowledge to other people, convincing them that you know—you know more than anybody. It will be useful for that, but in real life . . . If you are talking about love, you will be able to talk much from the memory that I have said to you, but when the question arises—you fall in love— then you will act out of your self—not what you have heard—because nobody can use a dead memory when a real situation arises.

I have heard an anecdote:

One day, while in the jungle, an explorer ran into a tribe of cannibals who were getting ready to sit down to their favourite dish. The head of the tribe, surprisingly, spoke excellent English. When questioned as to the reason, he admitted to having spent a year at college in the United States.

'You have been to college,' exclaimed the horrified explorer, 'and you still eat human flesh?'

'Well, yes, I do,' admitted the chief. Then he added in a conciliatory tone, 'But, now, of course, I use a knife and fork.'

That will be all. If you make me only part of your memory, you will still go on being a cannibal but now you will use a knife and fork. That will be the only difference. But if you allow me to enter your innermost shrine of being, you listen totally—that is the meaning of listening totally—then forget about the computer and the memory, there is no need.

Your real examination is not going to be in any examination hall of some university. Your examination is going to be in the universe itself. There will be the proof of whether you listened to me or not. Suddenly, you will see that you are loving in a different way, that the situation is old but you are responding in a different way. Somebody is annoying you, but you are not annoyed. Somebody is trying to irritate you, but you are silent and tranquil. Somebody is insulting you, but somehow you are untouched.

You are like a lotus flower: in the water, untouched by it. Then you will realize what has happened being with me.

It is a transference of being, not a communication of knowledge.

ॐ

> *I would like to ask one of those short, funny questions which you use at the end of a lecture and to hear you say, 'This question is from Dheerendra.' If I continue meditating, will it come?*

Never. Then stop meditating. If you want questions, please don't meditate. If you meditate, all questions disappear, only the answer remains. If you want more questions to ask, stop meditating. Then you can go on asking a thousand and one questions.

And all are stupid and funny, so there is no need to be worried about it.

But of only one thing should you be aware: don't meditate! If you want to ask funny and stupid questions, don't meditate. And I say again, all questions are stupid and funny. If you meditate, they all will disappear: only silence remains. And silence is the answer.

Remember, either you have questions or you have answers. You never have both. When you have questions, you don't have the answer. I can give you the answer, but it will never reach you. By the time it reaches you, you will convert it into a thousand and one questions again. When you have questions, you have questions. When you have the answer—and I say *answer*, not answers, because there is only one answer to all questions, when you have the answer, questions do not arise.

Meditate, if you want the answer which answers all questions. Stop meditating if you want to go on asking questions.

Meditation is the answer.

✍

3. The Inside of the Inside

6. Sanyama is to be employed in stages.

7. These three—dharana, dhyan and samadhi—are internal compared to the five that precede them.

8. But the three are external compared to seedless samadhi.

9. Nirodh Parinam is the transformation of the mind in which the mind becomes permeated by the condition of Nirodh, which intervenes momentarily between an impression that is disappearing and the impression that is taking its place.

10. This flow becomes peaceful with repeated impressions.

I HAVE BEEN told that traditionally, there are two schools of thought in Germany. The industrial, practical northern part of the country has this philosophy: the situation is serious but not hopeless. In the southern part of Germany, more romantic and perhaps less practical, the philosophy seems to be: the situation is hopeless but not serious. If you ask me, the situation is neither—neither is it hopeless nor serious. And I am talking about the human situation.

The human situation looks serious because we have been taught and conditioned to be serious, for centuries. The human situation looks hopeless because we have been doing something with ourselves which is wrong. We have not yet found that to be natural is the goal, and all the goals that we have been taught make us more and more unnatural.

To be natural, to be just in tune with the cosmic law, is what Patanjali means by *sanyama*. To be natural and to be in tune with the cosmic law is *sanyama*. *Sanyama* is not anything forced upon you. *Sanyama* is not anything that comes from the outside. *Sanyama* is a flowering of your innermost nature. *Sanyama* is to become that which you already are. *Sanyama* is to come back to nature. How to come back to nature? And what is human nature? Unless you dig deep within your own being, you will never come to know what human nature is.

One has to move inwards; and the whole process of yoga is a pilgrimage, an inward journey. Step by step, in eight steps, Patanjali is bringing you home. The first five steps—*yam, niyam, anga, pranayam, pratyahar*—they help you to go deep in you beyond the body. The body is your first periphery, the first concentric circle of your existence. The second step is to go beyond the mind. The three internal steps of *dharana, dhyan, samadhi*, lead you beyond the mind. Beyond the body and beyond the mind is your nature, is your centre of being. That centre of being Patanjali calls seedless *samadhi*—*kaivalya*. That he calls to come face to face to your own grounding, to your own being, to come to know who you are.

So the whole process can be divided into three parts: first, how to transcend the body; second, how to transcend the mind; and third, how to fall into your own being.

We have been taught, almost all over the world, in every culture, in every country, in every climate, to seek goals somewhere outside ourselves. The goal may be money, the goal may be power, the goal may be prestige, or the goal may be God, heaven, it makes no difference: all the goals are outside you. And the real goal is to come to the source from where you come. Then the circle is complete.

Drop all the outer goals and move inwards. That's the message of yoga. Outer goals are just forced. You have just been taught somewhere to go. They never become natural; they cannot become natural.

I have heard an anecdote about G.K. Chesterton:

He was on a train, reading earnestly, when the conductor asked for his ticket. Frantically, Chesterton fumbled for it.

'Never mind, sir,' the conductor said reassuringly. 'I will come later on to punch it. I am certain you have it.'

'I know I have it,' Chesterton stammered, 'but what I want to know is, where in the world am I going?'

Where are you going? What's your destiny? You have been taught certain things to achieve. You have been made into an achiever. The mind has been manipulated, pushed and pulled. The mind has been controlled by the outside—by the parents, by the family, by the school, by society, by government. Everybody is trying to pull you outside your being, and they are trying to fix a goal for you; and you have fallen in the trap. And the goal is already there inside you.

There is nowhere to go. One has to realize oneself, already—who one is. And once you realize that, wherever you go, you will find your goal, because you carry your goal with yourself. Then wherever you go, you will have a deep contentment, a peace surrounding you, a coolness, a collectedness, a calm as a milieu that you carry around you as an aura. That's what Patanjali calls *sanyama*: a cool, collected, calm atmosphere that moves with you.

Wherever you go, you bring your own atmosphere with you, and everybody can feel it. Almost, it can be touched by others also, whether they become aware or not. Suddenly, if a man of *sanyama* comes close to you, suddenly you become aware of a certain calm breeze blowing near you, a fragrance coming from the unknown. It touches you, it pacifies you. It is like a beautiful lullaby. You were in turmoil, if a man of *sanyama* comes near you, suddenly, your turmoil subsides. You were angry, if a man of *sanyama* comes near you, your anger disappears. Because a man of sanyama is a magnetic force. On his wave, you start riding; on him, with him, you start moving higher than you can move alone.

So, in the East, we developed a beautiful tradition of going to people who have attained to *sanyama* and just sitting by their side. That's what we call *darshan*, that's what we call *satsang*: just going to a man of *sanyama* and just being near him. To the Western mind, sometimes, it looks almost absurd because sometimes the man may not even speak, he may be in silence. And people go on coming, they touch his feet, they sit by his side, they close their eyes . . . There is no conversation, there is no verbal communication, and they sit for hours; and then fulfilled, in some unknown way, they touch the feet in deep gratitude and they go back. And you can watch from their faces that something has been communicated; they have attained to something. And there has been no verbal communication— nothing visible has been given or taken. This is *satsang*: just being with a man of truth, with an authentic being, a man of *sanyama*.

Just by being close to him, something starts happening in you, something starts responding in you.

But the concept of the man of *sanyama* has also become very muddled because people started to do it from the outside. People started to still themselves from the outside, to practise a certain calmness, a certain silence, to force themselves into a particular pattern and discipline. They will look almost like a man of *sanyama*. They will look almost, but they will not be: and when you go near them, their appearance may be of silence, but if you sit near them silently, you will not feel any silence. Deep down the turmoil is hidden. They are like volcanoes. On the surface, everything is quiet: deep down, the volcano is getting ready to explode any moment.

Remember this: never try to force anything upon you. That is the way to get divided, that's the way to become hopeless, and that's the way to miss the point. Your innermost being has to flow through you. You are only to remove the hindrances on the path. Nothing new is to be added to you. In fact, something minus, and you will be perfect. Something plus—no. You are already perfect. Something more is there than the spring, some rocks on the path. Minus those rocks, and you are perfect and the flow is attained. These eight steps, *ashtang*, of Patanjali are nothing but a methodological way of removing the rocks.

But why does man become so obsessed with an outer discipline? There must be a cause to it, a reason for it. The reason is there. The reason is that to force anything from the outside seems easier, cheap, at no cost. It is as if you are not beautiful, but you can purchase a beautiful mask from the market and you can put it on your face. Cheap, not costly, and you can deceive others a little bit. Not long, because a mask is a dead thing and a dead thing can have an appearance of beauty, but it cannot be really beautiful. In fact, you have become more ugly than you were before. Whatsoever your original face was, was at least alive, radiating life, intelligence. Now you have a dead mask, and you are hiding behind it.

People become interested in cultivating *sanyama* from the outside. You are a man of anger: to attain to a state of no anger much effort will be needed, and long is the journey, and you will have to pay for it. But just to force yourself, repress anger, is easier. In fact, you can use your energy of anger in repressing anger—immediately. There is no problem because anybody who is a man of anger can easily conquer anger. The only one thing is he has to turn the anger upon himself. First he was angry with others, now he has to be angry with himself and suppress the anger. But if you look into his eyes, anger will be there, lurking like a shadow.

And, remember, to be angry sometimes is not bad, but to suppress anger and to remain angry constantly is very dangerous. That is the difference between hatred and hate. When you flare up in anger, there is hate, but it is momentary. It comes and it goes. Nothing much to be worried about it. When you suppress anger, then hate disappears and hatred arises, which becomes a permanent style of your life. The repressed anger continuously affects you—your behaviour, your relationship. Now it is not that you sometimes become angry, now you are all the time angry. Your anger is not addressed to anybody now: it has become unaddressed, just a quality of your being. Now it clings to you. You cannot say exactly with whom you are angry, because in the past you have been accumulating anger. Now, it has become a reservoir. You are simply angry.

This is bad; this is chronic. First the anger was just a flare-up, something happened. It was situational. It was like when small children become angry: they flare up like a flame and then they subside, and immediately the storm is gone and the silence is there and they are again loving and beautiful. But, by and by, the more you suppress anger, anger enters into your bones, into your blood. It circulates within you. It moves in your breathing. Then, whatsoever you do, you do in anger. Even if you love a person, you love in an angry way. Aggression is there: destructiveness is there. You may not bring it up, but it is always there. And it becomes a great rock.

To force anything from the outside seems, in the beginning, very cheap, but in the end, it proves very fatal.

And people find it cheap because there are experts who go on telling them how to do it. A child is born and parents become the experts. They are not. They have not solved their own problems yet. If they really love the child, they will not force the same pattern on him.

But who loves? Nobody knows what love is.

They start forcing their pattern, the same old pattern in which they are caught. They are not even aware what they are doing. They themselves are caught in the same pattern and their whole life has been a life of misery, and now they are giving the same pattern to their children. Innocent children, not knowing what is right and what is wrong, will become victims.

And these experts who are not experts, because they don't know anything—they have not solved any problem themselves—simply take it for granted that because, just because, they have given birth to a child, they have become, in a certain way, authoritative, and they start moulding the soft child into a fixed pattern. And the child has to follow them; the child is helpless. By the time he becomes aware, he is already caught, trapped. Then there are schools, universities, and a thousand and one ways of conditioning all around, and all sorts of experts, and everybody pretending that he knows. Nobody seems to know.

Beware of the experts. Take your life in your own hands if you want to reach some day to your innermost core. Don't listen to the experts; you have listened long enough.

I have heard a small anecdote:

An efficiency expert was checking a government bureau and came to an office where two young men were seated on opposite sides of a desk, neither occupied with work.

'What are your duties?' the expert asked one.

'I have been here six months, and I have not been given any duties yet,' the man replied.

'And your duties?' the efficiency expert asked the other man.

'I too have been here for six months and have not been given any duties yet,' he replied.

'Well, one of you must go,' snubbed the expert. 'This is an obvious instance of duplication.'

Two persons doing the same duty—of not doing anything.

The expert always thinks in terms of knowledge. Go to a wise man. He does not think in terms of knowledge. He looks at you through his knowing eyes. The world is ruled too much by experts, and the world has almost forgotten to go to the wise men. And the difference is the expert is as ordinary as you are. The only difference between you and the expert is that he has accumulated some dead information. He knows more than you know, but his information is not his own realization. He has just accumulated it from the outside, and he goes on giving advice to you.

Seek, search for a wise man. That is the search for the guru. In the East, people travel for thousands of miles to seek and search for somebody who has really come to know, and to be with him, to be with the man of *sanyama*— one who has attained, who has not cultivated, who has grown, who has flowered in his inner being. The flower is not borrowed from the outside. It is an inner flowering.

Remember, Patanjali's *sanyama* is not the concept of ordinary cultivation. It is the concept of flowering, of helping and allowing that which is hidden in you to be manifested. You are already carrying the seed. The seed only needs a right soil. A little care, a loving care, and it will sprout, and it will come one day to flower. And the fragrance that was carried by the seed will be spread to the winds, and the winds will carry it to all the directions.

A man of *sanyama* cannot hide himself. He tries. He cannot hide himself, because the winds will continuously carry his fragrance. He can go to a cave in the mountains and sit there, and people will start coming to him there. Somehow, in some unknown way, those who are growing, those who are intelligent, they will find him. He need not seek them; they will seek him.

Can you watch something similar in your own being, because then it will be easy to understand the sutras? You love somebody, really; and, you show love to somebody. Have you watched the difference? Somebody comes, a guest. You really welcome. It is a flowering; from your very being you welcome him. It is not only a welcome to your home, it is a welcome to your heart. And then some other guest comes, and you welcome him because you have to welcome. Have you watched the difference between the two?

When you really welcome, you are one flow—the welcome is total. When you don't really welcome, and you are simply following etiquette, manners, you are not one flow; and if the guest is perceptive, he will immediately turn back. He will not enter your house. If he is *really* perceptive, he can immediately see the contradiction in you. Your extended hand for a handshake is not really extended. The energy in it is not moving towards the guest; the energy is being withheld. Only a dead hand has been spread out.

You are a contradiction whenever you are following anything outer, just following a discipline. It is not true; you are not in it.

Remember, whatsoever you do—if you are doing it at all—do it totally. If you don't want to do it at all, don't do it—then don't do it totally. The totalness has to be remembered because that totalness is the most significant thing. If you continuously go on doing things in which you are contradictory, inconsistent, in which a part of you moves and another part doesn't move, you are destroying your inner flowering. By and by, you will become a plastic flower—with no fragrance, with no life.

It happened:

Mulla Nasruddin, on leaving a party, said to his hostess, 'Thank you very much for inviting me. It is the very nicest party I have ever been invited to in all my life.' And the party was very ordinary.

Somewhat taken aback, the hostess exclaimed, 'Oh, don't say that.'

To which the Mulla replied, 'But I do say that. I always say that.'

Then it is meaningless. Then it is absolutely meaningless.

Don't live a life of mere manners, don't live a life of mere etiquette. Live an authentic life.

I know the life of etiquette, manner, is comfortable, convenient; but it is poisonous. It kills you slowly, slowly. The life of authenticity is not so convenient and comfortable. It is risky, it is dangerous—but it is real, and the danger is worth it. And you will never repent for it. Once you start enjoying the real life, the real feeling, the real flow of your energy, and you are not divided and split, then you will understand that if everything is to be staked for it, it is worth it. For a single moment of real life, your whole unreal life can be staked, and it is worth—because in that single moment, you would have known what life is and its destiny. And your whole long life of a hundred years, you will simply live on the surface, always afraid of the depth, and you will miss the whole opportunity.

This is the hopelessness that we have created all around us; living and not living at all, doing things we never intended to do, being in relationships we never wanted to be, following a profession which has never been a call to you. Being false in a thousand and one ways, and how do you expect that out of this falsity, layer upon layer, you can know what life is? It is because of your falsity you are missing it. It is because of your falsity you cannot make the contact with the living stream of life.

And, sometimes, when you become aware of it, a second problem arises. Whenever people become aware of the falsity of life, they immediately move to the opposite extreme. That is another trap of the mind because if you move from one falsity to the exact opposite, you will move to another falsity again. Somewhere in between, somewhere between the two opposites, is the real.

Sanyama means balance. It means absolute balance, not moving to the extremes, remaining just in the middle. When you are neither a rightist nor a leftist, when you are neither a socialist nor an individualist, when you are neither this nor that, suddenly, in between, the flowering, the flowering of *sanyama*.

It happened that Mulla Nasruddin was suffering from a very deep-rooted fear. It had almost become an obsession. I advised him to go to a psychiatrist. Then one day, after a few weeks, when I saw him, I asked, 'I understand that you have been going to the psychiatrist I suggested to you. Do you think it has helped you?'

'Certainly it has. Only a few weeks ago, when the phone rang, I was deadly afraid to answer it.'

That was his fear, always. The ringing of the phone, and he will start trembling. Who knows what is the message? Who knows who is calling him? 'Only a few weeks ago, when the phone rang, I was deadly afraid to answer it.'

'And now?' I asked.

He said, 'And now? I go right ahead and answer it—whether it rings or not.'

You can move from one extreme to another, from one falsity to another falsity, from one fear to another fear. You can move from the marketplace to the monastery. Those are the polarities. The people who live in the marketplace are unbalanced, and the people who live in the monasteries are also unbalanced, on the other extreme, but both are lopsided.

Sanyama means balance. That's what I mean by *sanyas*, to be balanced, to be in the marketplace, and yet not be of it, to be in the bazaar but to not allow the bazaar to be in you. If your mind can remain free from the marketplace, you can be in the marketplace and there is no problem, you can move to the monastery and live alone; but if the bazaar follows inside you . . . which is bound to follow because the bazaar is not really outside—it is in the buzzing thoughts, in the inner traffic noise of the thoughts. It is going to follow you. How can you leave yourself here and escape somewhere else? You will go with yourself, and wherever you go, you will be the same.

So don't try to escape from situations. Rather, try to become more and more aware. Change the inner climate and don't be worried about the outer situations. Insist continuously on it, because the cheaper is always alluring.

It says, 'Because you are worried in the market, escape to the monastery and all worries will disappear: because worries are because of the business, because of the market, because of the relationship.' No, worries are not because of the market, worries are not because of the family, worries are not because of the relationship: worries are because of you. These are just excuses. If you go to the monastery, these worries will find some new objects to hang to, but the worries will continue.

Just look at your mind, in what a mess it is. And this mess is not created by the situations. This mess is in you. Situations, at the most, work as excuses.

Sometime, do one experiment. You think people make you angry, then go for a twenty-one day silence. Remain silent and you will suddenly become aware that many times in the day, for no reason at all—because now there is nobody to make you angry—you become angry. You think because you come across a beautiful woman or a man, that's why you become sexual? You are wrong. Go for a twenty-one day silence. Remain alone and you will find many times, suddenly, for no reason at all, sexuality arises. It is within *you*.

Two women were talking. I have simply overheard them; excuse my trespass.

Mistress Brown, very annoyed: 'Look here, Mistress Green. Mistress Gray told me that you told her the secret I told you not to tell her.'

Mistress Green: 'Oh! The mean creature! And I told her not to tell you that I told her.'

Mistress Brown: 'Well, look here, don't tell her that I told you she told me.'

This is the traffic noise that goes on continuously in the mind. This has to be stilled, not by any force but by understanding.

ॐ

The first sutra:

> *Sanyama is to be employed in stages.*

Patanjali is not for sudden enlightenment: and sudden enlightenment is not for everybody. It is rare, it is exceptional; and Patanjali has a very scientific outlook, he does not bother for the exceptional. He discovers the rule, and the exceptional simply proves the rule, nothing else. And the exceptional can take care of itself: there is no need to think about it. The ordinary, the ordinary human being, grows only in stages, step by step, because for a sudden enlightenment, tremendous courage is needed, which is not available.

And, for sudden enlightenment, there is such a risk in it—one can go mad or one can become enlightened. Both the possibilities remain open because it is so sudden that the mechanism of your body and mind is not ready for it. It can shatter you completely.

Patanjali does not talk about it. In fact, he insists that the *sanyama* should be attained in stages so that, by and by, you move, in small doses you grow, and before you take another step, you have become ready and prepared for it. Enlightenment, for Patanjali, does not take you unawares. Because it is such a tremendous event, you may be so shocked—shocked to death or shocked to madness— he simply debars any talk about it. He does not pay any attention to it.

That is the difference between Patanjali and Zen. Zen is for the exceptional: Patanjali is the rule. If Zen disappears from the world, nothing will be lost because that exceptional can always take care of itself. But if Patanjali disappears from the world, much will be lost because he is the rule. He is simply for the common, ordinary human being—for all. A Tilopa may take the jump, or a Bodhidharma may take a jump, and disappear. These are adventurers, people who enjoy risk, but that is not the way of everybody. You need a staircase to go up and to go down: you simply don't jump out of balconies. And there is no need to take that risk while one can move gracefully.

Zen is a little eccentric because the whole point is of the unique experience. The whole point is of the exceptional, the rare: in a way, the non-ordinary. Patanjali, in that way, moves on plain ground. For the common humanity, he is a great help.

He says, *Sanyama is to be employed in stages.* Don't be in a hurry, move slowly, grow slowly, so everything becomes solid before you take another step. After each growth, let there be an interval. In that interval, whatsoever you have attained is absorbed, digested, becomes part of your being . . . then go ahead. There is no need to run because in running, you can come to a point for which you are not ready, and if you are not ready, it is dangerous.

The greedy mind would like to attain everything *now*. People come to me and they say, 'Why don't you give us something which can make us suddenly enlightened?' But these are exactly the people who are not ready. If they were ready, they would have patience. If they were ready, they would say, 'Whenever it comes. We are not in a hurry: we can wait.' They are not the real people: they are greedy people. In fact, they don't know what they are asking. They are inviting the sky. You will burst, you won't be able to contain it.

ॐ

Patanjali says, *Sanyama is to be employed in stages*, and these eight stages he has described.

> *These three . . .*

The three that we discussed the other day . . .

> —*Dharana, dhyan, and samadhi—are internal compared to the five that precede them.*

We have discussed those five stages.

These three are internal compared to the five that have preceded them . . .

> *But the three are external compared to seedless samadhi.*

If you compare them with *yam*, *niyam*, *asan*, *pranayam*, *pratyahar*, they are internal, but if you compare with the experience, the ultimate experience of a buddha or Patanjali, they are yet external. They are just in between. First you transcend the body, those are the external steps: then you transcend the mind, these are internal steps: but when you reach to your being, even that which was internal now, will look external. Even that was not internal enough. Your mind is not internal enough. It is more internal than the body. It is external if you become a witness: then you can watch your own thoughts. When you can watch your own thoughts, your thoughts become external. They become objects: you are the watcher.

The *seedless samadhi* means: when there is going to be no birth any more, when there is going to be no coming back to the world any more, when there is going to be no entry again in time. The *seedless* means the seed of desire is burned completely.

When you move, even towards yoga, when you start the journey inwards, that too is still a desire—desire to achieve oneself, desire to achieve peace, bliss, desire to achieve truth. It is still desire. When you attain the first *samadhi* . . . After *dharana*, concentration; *dhyan*, contemplation; when you come to *samadhi*, where subject and object become one, even there, a slight shadow of desire is present—the desire to know the truth, the desire to become one, the desire to know God—or whatsoever you name it. Still that desire, very subtle, almost invisible, almost as if it is not: but still it is there. It has to be there because you have been using it all throughout the way. Now that desire also has to be dropped.

Samadhi has also to be dropped. Meditation becomes complete when meditation has to be dropped . . . when meditation can be dropped. When you forget all about meditation and you drop it, when there is no need to meditate, when there is no need to go anywhere—neither outside nor inside—when all journeying stops, then desire disappears.

Desire is the seed. First it moves you outwards: then, if you are intelligent enough to understand that you are moving in a wrong direction, it starts moving you inwards: but the desire is still there. The same desire, feeling frustrated outside, starts searching inside. That desire has to be dropped.

After *samadhi*, even *samadhi* has to be dropped. Then

the *seedless samadhi* arises. That is the ultimate. It arises not because you desired it, because if you desire, it will not be seedless. That has to be understood. It arises only because understanding the futility of desire itself—even the desire to go in the very understanding of the futility of desire, desire disappears. You cannot desire the *seedless samadhi*. When desire disappears, suddenly, the *seedless samadhi* is there. It has nothing to do with your effort. This is the happening.

Up to now, up to *samadhi*, there is effort: because effort needs desire, motivation. When desire disappears, effort also disappears. When desire disappears, there is no motivation to do anything—neither is there any motivation to do nor is there any motivation to be anything. Total emptiness, nothingness, what Buddha calls *shunya*, arises—on its own accord. And that's the beauty of it: untouched by your desire, uncorrupted by your motivation, it is purity itself, it is innocence itself. This is *seedless samadhi*.

Now, there will no longer be any birth. Buddha used to tell his disciples, 'When you come to *samadhi*, become alert. Cling to *samadhi* so that you can be a help to people.' Because if you don't cling to *samadhi*, and the *seedless samadhi* appears, you are gone, gone forever—*gate, gate, para gate*—Gone, gone, gone forever. Then you cannot help. You must have heard the word 'bodhisattva'. I have given the word to many sanyasis. Bodhisattva means one who has come to *samadhi* and is denying *seedless samadhi*, is clinging to *samadhi* because while he clings to *samadhi*, he can help people, he can still be there, at least one chain with the world is still there.

There is a story that Buddha comes to the ultimate heaven,

doors open, and he is invited, but he stands outside. The *devas* tell him, 'Come in. We have been waiting so long for you.' But he says, 'How can I come in right now? There are many who need me. I will stand at the door and help to show people the door. I will be the last to enter. When everybody has entered the door, when there is nobody else left outside, then I will enter. If I enter right now, with my entry, the door will be lost again: and there are millions who are struggling. They are just coming closer and closer. I will stand outside; I am not going to enter, because you will have to keep the door open while I stand here. You will have to wait for me, and while you are waiting, the door will be there, open, and I can show people this is the door.'

This is the state of bodhisattva. Bodhisattva means one who has already come to the door of being a buddha. In essence, he is ready to disappear into the whole, but he resists for compassion. He clings to it. The last desire, to help people—that too is a desire—keeps him in existence. It is very difficult, it is almost impossible, when all the chains are broken from the world, just to depend on a very fragile relationship of compassion—almost impossible. But those are the few moments—when somebody comes to the state of bodhisattva and stays there—those are the few moments when the door is open for the whole of humanity, to look at the door, to realize the door, to recognize, and to enter it.

These three—*dharana*, *dhyan*, *samadhi*—are internal compared to the five that preceded them, but the three are external compared to *seedless samadhi*.

ॐ

> *Nirodh parinam is the transformation of the mind in which the mind becomes permeated by the condition of nirodh, which intervenes momentarily between an impression that is disappearing and the impression that is taking its place.*

This sutra is very, very significant for you because you can immediately use it. Patanjali calls it *nirodh*. *Nirodh* means a momentary suspension of the mind, a momentary state of no-mind. It is happening to you all, but it is very subtle and the moment is very small. Unless you are a little more aware, you will not be able to see it. First let me describe what it is.

Whenever a thought appears in the mind, the mind is covered with it like a cloud appears in the sky. But no thought can be permanent. The very nature of thought is to be non-permanent: one thought comes, it goes; another thought comes and replaces it. Between these two thoughts there is a very subtle interval. One thought goes, another has not come yet: that is the moment of *nirodh*—subtle interval when you are thoughtless. One cloud has passed, another has not come yet, and the sky is open. You can look at it.

Just sitting silently, watch. Thoughts go on coming like traffic on the road. One car has passed, another is coming— but between the two, there is a gap and the road is vacant. Soon the other will come and the road will again be full and will not be empty. If you can look between the gap that exists between two thoughts, you are for a moment in the same state as when somebody comes to realize *samadhi*—a momentary *samadhi*, just a glimpse. Immediately, it will be filled by another thought which is already on the way.

Watch. Watch carefully. One thought going, another coming, and the gap between: in that gap, you are exactly in the same state as one who has attained to *samadhi*. But your state is just a momentary phenomenon. Patanjali calls it *nirodh*. It is momentary, dynamic, it is changing all the time. It is a flux-like thing: one wave going, another coming; between the two . . . no wave. Just try to watch it.

This is one of the most significant meditations. There is no need to do anything else. You can just sit silently and you can go on watching. Just look in the gap. In the beginning, it will be difficult. By and by, you will become more alert and you will not miss the gaps. Don't pay attention to the thoughts. Focus yourself on the gap, not on the thoughts. Focus yourself when the road is vacant and nobody is passing. Change your gestalt. Ordinarily, we focus on thoughts and we don't focus in between.

It happened once. A great yoga master was teaching about *nirodh* to his disciples. He had a blackboard. On the blackboard, with a white chalk, he made a very small point, just visible, and then he asked his disciples, 'What do you see?' They all said, 'A small white point.' The master laughed. He said, 'Nobody can see this blackboard? All are seeing only the small white point?'

Nobody has seen the blackboard. The blackboard was there, the white dot was there, but they all looked at the white dot.

Change the gestalt.

Have you looked in children's books? There are pictures, pictures which are very, very meaningful to be understood.

In a certain picture there is a young woman, you can see it, but in the same lines, in the same picture, there is hiding an old woman. If you go on looking, go on looking, suddenly, the young woman disappears and you see the old woman's face. Then you go on looking at the old woman's face—suddenly, it disappears and again the young woman's face appears. You cannot see both together: that is impossible. You can see one face one time, another face another time. Once you have seen both the faces, you know very well that the other face is also there, but still you cannot see it together. And the mind is constantly changing, so one time you see the young face, another time you see the old face.

The gestalt changes from the old to the young, from the young to the old, from the old to the young, but you cannot focus on both. So, when you focus on thoughts, you cannot focus on the gaps. The gaps are always there. Focus on the gaps, and suddenly you will become aware that gaps are there and thoughts are disappearing: and in those gaps the first glimpses of *samadhi* will be attained.

And that taste is needed in order to go on because whatsoever I say, whatsoever Patanjali says, can only become meaningful to you when you have already tasted something of it. If once you know the gap is blissful, a tremendous bliss descends—just for a moment, then it disappears—then you know if this gap can become permanent, if this gap can become my nature, then this bliss will be available as a continuum. Then you start working hard.

This is *nirodh parinam*: *Nirodh parinam is the transformation of the mind in which the mind becomes permeated by the condition of nirodh, which intervenes*

*momentarily between an impression that is disappearing
and the impression that is taking its place.*

Just ten years ago, an inventory was made of the Imperial
Japanese jewels. The royal treasure has been kept in a
guarded building called the Soshuen. For 900 years the
jewels had rested in that palace. When a string of amber
beads was examined, one bead in the centre of the string
appeared to be different from the others. The accumulated
dust of centuries was washed off the beads and the centre
stone was examined with deep curiosity. The examiners
found a treasure within a treasure. The special bead was
not made of common amber as were the other beads. It
was a high quality pearl of pink-green colour. For hundreds
of years, the unique pearl had been mistaken for a piece of
amber, but no longer.

No matter how long we have lived in a mistaken identity,
self-examination can reveal our true and tranquil nature.

Once you have a glimpse of the reality that you are,
then all false identities which have existed for centuries
suddenly disappear. Now, no longer can you be deceived
by those identities. This *nirodh parinam* gives you the first
glimpse of your real nature. It gives you a glimpse, behind
the layers of dust, of the real pearl. The layers of dust are
nothing but layers of thought, impressions, imaginations,
dreams, desires—all thoughts.

Once you can have one glimpse, you are already
converted. This I call conversion. Not when a Hindu
becomes a Christian, not when a Christian becomes a
Hindu, that is not a conversion. That is moving from one
prison to another prison. The conversion is when you

move from thought to no-thought, when you move from mind to no-mind. The conversion is when you look in *nirodh parinam*, when you look between two thoughts and suddenly your reality is revealed—almost like lightning. Then again there is darkness, but you are not the same. You have seen something you cannot forget now. Now you will be searching again and again.

ॐ

This is what the following sutra says:

> *This flow becomes peaceful with repeated impressions.*

If again and again you fall in the gap, if again and again you taste the experience, if again and again you look through the *nirodh*—cessation of the mind—without thought you look into your own being: this flow becomes peaceful, this flow becomes natural, this flow becomes spontaneous. You attain, you begin to attain, your own treasure. First, as glimpses, small gaps; then bigger gaps, then still bigger. Then one day it happens the last thought is gone and no other thought comes. You are in deep silence, eternal silence. That's the goal.

It is hard, arduous, but available.

Tradition has it that when Jesus was crucified, just before he died, a soldier pierced his side with a spear, just to see whether he is dead or still alive. He was still alive. He opened his eyes. Looked at the soldier, and said, 'Friend, there is a shorter road to my heart than that.' He has pierced his heart with a spear, and Jesus says, 'Friend, there is a shorter road to *my* heart than that.'

For centuries, people have wondered what he really meant. A thousand and one explanations are possible because the sentence is very cryptic, but the way I look into it and the meaning that I think into it is that if you go into your own heart, that is the shortest, the most short cut way to reach to Jesus' heart. If you go into your own heart, if you go withinwards, you will come closer to Jesus.

And, whether Jesus is alive or not, you have to look withinwards, you have to seek the source of your own life; and then you will know that Jesus can never be dead. He is eternal life. He may disappear from this body on the cross; he will appear somewhere else. He may not appear anywhere else, but then too he will remain for eternity into the heart of the whole.

When Jesus said, 'Friend, there is a shorter road to my heart than that,' he meant, 'Go withinwards. Look into your own nature, and you will find me there. The kingdom of God is within you.' And it is eternal. It is unending life; it is deathless life.

If you look into *nirodh*, you will look into deathless life, life that has no beginning and no end.

And once you have tasted that ambrosia, that elixir, then nothing else can become the object of your desire— nothing else. Then that becomes the object of desire. That desire can lead you up to *samadhi*, and then that desire has also to be left, that desire has also to be dropped. It has done its work. It gave you a momentum, it brought you to your very door of being; now that has to be dropped also.

Once you drop it, you are there no more . . . only God is. This is *seedless samadhi*.

✠

4. Be a Seed

> *Osho, I have heard that Patanjali and Lao Tzu came to a stream. Patanjali began to cross the stream by walking on the surface of the water. Lao Tzu stood on the bank and called him to come back. 'What's the matter?' Patanjali inquired. 'That is no way to cross a stream,' said Lao Tzu, and led him to a place where the water was shallow, and they waded across together.*

THIS IS FROM Yatri. The story is true, but Yatri, you have missed the most important point in it. Let me tell you the whole story again:

I have heard that Patanjali and Lao Tzu came to a stream. Patanjali began to cross the stream by walking on the surface of the water. Lao Tzu stood on the bank and called him to come back.

'What's the matter?' Patanjali inquired.

Said Lao Tzu, 'There is no need to cross the stream, because this shore is the other shore.'

That's the whole emphasis of Lao Tzu: there is no need to

go anywhere; the other shore is here. There is no need to do anything. The only need is just to be. Effort is irrelevant because you are already that which you can ever be. Go nowhere. Follow no path. Seek nothing. Because wherever you will go, the very going is missing the point because everything is available here already.

I will tell you another story, one of the most important stories in the world of human consciousness. The story is concerned with Zarathustra, another Lao Tzu, who believed in being natural, who believed in being easy, who believed in being just to be:

Once, when Vishtaspa, king of Persia, was returning from a victorious campaign, he came near the place where Zarathustra lived. He decided to visit the mystic. The king said to Zarathustra, 'I have come that you may explain to me the laws of nature and the universe. I cannot tarry as I am on my way home from a war and important matters of state await me at my palace.'

Looking at the king, Zarathustra smiled and took a grain of wheat from the earth and gave it to him. 'In this small grain of wheat', he declared, 'are contained all the laws of the universe and the forces of nature.'

The king was much astonished by this answer, which he didn't understand, and when he saw smiles on the faces of those around him, he was angry and threw the grain upon the ground, thinking that he was being mocked. And to Zarathustra he said, 'I was foolish to waste my time by coming here to see you.'

Years passed. The king was successful as a ruler and a warrior, and led a life of luxury and apparent contentment, but at night when he went to bed, strange thoughts came into his mind and troubled him: 'I live in luxury and abundance in this splendid palace, but how long shall I enjoy this—this abundance, this power, this wealth—and what will happen to me when I die? Can my power and my riches save me from illness and death? Is everything lost with the coming of death?'

No one in the palace could answer these questions but, meanwhile, the fame of Zarathustra grew. So putting aside his pride, he dispatched a great caravan of treasure to Zarathustra and with it an invitation and a request. 'I regret,' he wrote, 'that when I was impatient and thoughtless in my youth, I asked you to explain the great problems of existence in a few minutes of time. I have changed and do not want the impossible now, but I am still deeply interested to know the laws of the universe and the forces of nature, even more so than when I was a young man. Come to my palace, I pray you. Or if that is not possible, then send to me the best of your disciples that he may teach me all that he can about these questions.'

After an interval, the caravan and the messengers returned. These told the king that they had found Zarathustra, who sent him greeting, but returned the proffered treasure. The treasure, Zarathustra had said, was of no use to him because he has attained to the ultimate treasure. Moreover, Zarathustra had sent the king a gift wrapped in a leaf and had asked the messengers to tell him that this was the teacher who could teach him everything.

The king opened it and found the same grain again— the same grain of wheat that Zarathustra had given him before. He thought there must be something mysterious and magical in it, so he put it in a golden box and hid it among his treasures. Almost every day he looked at it expecting some miracle to happen, such as the turning of the grain of wheat into something or someone that would teach him all he wished to know.

Months went by, and then years, but nothing happened. At last the king lost patience and said, 'It seems that Zarathustra has deceived me again. Either he is making a mockery of me or else he does not know the answers to my questions, but I will show him that I can find the answers without his help.' So the king sent a caravan to a great Indian mystic, Tshengrengacha, to whom came disciples from all over the world, and with the caravan went the same messengers and the same treasure that he had once sent to Zarathustra.

After many months, the messengers returned from India with the philosopher, but the philosopher said to him, 'I am honoured to be your teacher but in frankness must tell you that I come chiefly to your country that I may meet the great Zarathustra.'

Then the king took the golden box containing the grain of wheat and answered, 'I asked Zarathustra to teach me. See, this is what he sent me. Here is the teacher who shall teach me the laws of the universe and the forces of nature. Is this not ridiculous?'

The philosopher looked long at the grain of wheat, and silence fell upon the palace while he meditated. At length he said, 'I do not regret my many months of journeying, for now I know that Zarathustra is in truth the great teacher that I have long believed him to be. This tiny grain of wheat can indeed teach us the laws of the universe and the forces of nature, for it contains them in itself *right now*. You must not keep the grain of wheat in its golden box. You are missing the whole point.

'If you plant this little grain in the earth, where it belongs, in contact with the soil, the rain, the air, the sunshine, and the light of the moon and the stars, then like a universe in itself, it will begin to grow bigger and bigger. Likewise you, if you would grow in knowledge and understanding, must leave your artificial life and go where you will be close to all the forces of nature and of the universe, to the sum total of things. Just as inexhaustible sources of energy are ever flowing towards the grain planted in the earth, so will innumerable sources of knowledge open and flow towards you till you become one with nature and the organic universe. If you watch the growth of this seed of grain, you will find that there is an indestructible and mysterious power in it—the power of life. The grain disappears, and in that disappearance, there is victory over death.'

'All that you say is true,' answered the king, 'yet in the end the plant will wither and die and will be dissolved into the earth.'

'But not,' said the philosopher, 'until it has done an act of creation and has turned itself into hundreds of grain, each like the first. The tiny grain disappeared as it grew into a plant, and you too as you grow must turn yourself into something and someone else. Life always creates more life, truth more abundant truth, the seed more abundant seeds. The only art one needs to know is the art how to die. Then one is reborn. I propose that we journey to Zarathustra himself that he may teach us more of these things.'

In a few days, they came to the garden of Zarathustra. His only book was the great book of nature, and he taught his disciples to read in it. The two visitors learned another great truth in Zarathustra's garden that life and work, leisure and study, are one and the same: that the right way to live is a simple, natural life—a creative life within which individual growth is a single, total dynamism. They spent a year in the garden, learning to read the laws of existence and of life from the vast book of nature. At the end of that time, the king returned to his own city and asked Zarathustra to set out systematically the essence of his great teaching. Zarathustra did so, and the result was the great book of *Zend-Avesta*, the great book of the Parsis.

This long story is the whole story of how a man becomes God, how that which you are hiding within yourself can become revealed.

Be a seed. You are, but you may be still in a gold box, imprisoned. Fall into the earth, where you belong, and be ready to die into the earth. Don't be afraid to die, because all those who fear death are preventing themselves from life. Death is nothing but the door to life. The first acquaintance with life is death, so those who are afraid of death are barring themselves against life. Then they will remain secure in a gold box, but then they will not grow. Fearing death, they will not be able to resurrect themselves. In fact, their life in the gold box will be virtually nothing but death.

Death in the soil, in the earth, is just a beginning, not the end, but remaining in a gold box is the very end. There is no beginning in it.

You are a seed. There is no need to go anywhere. All that you need is ready to come to you, but the shell of the seed needs to be broken. The ego needs to dissolve into the earth; the ego needs to die into the earth. Immediately, the whole universe starts converging on you. Suddenly, you see that which you are always meant to be. The very destiny starts growing in you.

In fact, this shore is the other shore. There is no need to go anywhere. All that you need is to go within. All that you need is to take a jump into your own being, to be in tune with yourself. Lao Tzu would not show a way how to go to the other shore.

We can manage the story in a different way. Let there be three persons: Patanjali, Buddha, Lao Tzu. Patanjali will try to walk on the surface of the water—he can. He is a great scientist of the inner world of consciousness. He knows how to defy gravity, Buddha will say what Yatri says in the story. Buddha will say, 'This is no way to cross the stream. Come, I will show you a place where there is no need to do such hard work. Easy is the way. The stream is shallow: we just have to walk a few hundred yards and you can walk in the shallow stream. There is no need to learn this great art. This can be done so easily.' Buddha will say this. And Lao Tzu? He will laugh, and he will say to Buddha and Patanjali, 'What are you doing? If you leave this shore, you will go astray because this is the other shore. Here, this very moment, everything is as it should be. There is nowhere to go. Seeker of truth, follow no path, because all paths lead here, the truth is here.'

Lao Tzu says simply relax into yourself. It is not a journey; it is simply a let-go. No preparation is needed because it is not a journey. As you are, just as you are, relax. Relax into your nature. Drop all nonsense about gold boxes—prisons of morality, prisons of concepts, philosophies, religions. Drop all that rubbish. Don't be afraid of the earth and don't ask for heaven. Drop into the earth. Don't be afraid that your hands will become soiled. Fall into nature because only there, in fact, you belong, to the sum total of things.

Zarathustra did well. He was not mocking the king. He was a simple man, and because the king had himself said that he cannot waste much time and he has great affairs waiting at the palace and he has to go soon, that's why Zarathustra gave a symbolic sign, the seed. But he missed the whole point. He could not understand what type of message this is. Zarathustra had given him the whole *Zend-Avesta* in that seed: nothing remains. That is the whole message of the true religion. All else is just commentary.

That day Zarathustra gave the seed, he did the same as Buddha did when he gave the flower to Mahakashyap. With that seed, Zarathustra had given something more than the flower. Try to understand these symbols.

Buddha gives the flower. Flower is the end. It can be given only to a Mahakashyap, who has come to the very end. Zarathustra gave the seed. Seed is the beginning. It can be given to one who is just beginning to seek, who is just inquiring, who is just trying to find the way, who is groping in the dark. Buddha's flower cannot be given to everybody and anybody; a Mahakashyap is needed. In fact, it can be given only to someone who does not need it. Mahakashyap is one who does not need it. It can be given only to one who does not need it. Zarathustra's seed can be given to those who need it. And, what he said; he simply said, 'Become a seed. You are a seed. Hidden is God within you. But don't go anywhere else.'

Zarathustra's religion is one of the most natural religions: to accept life as it is, to live life as it is. Don't ask the impossible. Take it easy. Look all around. The truth is present; only you are absent. This shore is the other shore; there is no other shore. This life is the life; there is no other life.

But you can live this life in two ways: at the minimum, or at the optimum. If you live at the minimum, you live like a seed. If you live like a flower, you live at the optimum. Let your seed become the flower. It is the seed itself which will become the flower. It is you who will become the other shore. It is you who will become the truth.

Remember this. If you can remember this, just to be natural, you have understood all that is basic, all that is fundamental, all that is essential to be understood.

ॐ

What is the difference between Zazen-Zen and Patanjali's dhyan?

Patanjali's dhyan is a step; in his eight steps, *dhyan* is a step. In *zazen*, *dhyan* is the only step; there are no other steps. Patanjali believes in gradual growth. Zen, in sudden enlightenment. So what is only a step in Patanjali is all-in-all in Zen—just *dhyan* is enough, meditation is enough. Nothing else is needed. All else can be discarded. All else may be helpful but is not essential—in *zazen*, only meditation.

Patanjali gives you a complete system of all that is needed, of all requirements, from the very preliminary to the end. He gives you the whole teaching. It is not a sudden phenomenon; one has to grow into it by and by, slowly. As you go on growing and absorbing your growth, you become capable of further steps. Zen is for rare exceptions, for those few courageous souls who can risk all for nothing, who can risk everything without any expectations.

This is not possible for all. You move cautiously—and nothing is wrong in moving cautiously. If it comes natural to you, to move cautiously, you have to move cautiously. Then don't be a fool and don't try to jump. Listen to your nature. If you feel to be cautious is your nature, move cautiously. If you feel that to risk, to gamble, is your nature, don't be bothered with cautiousness, then don't be bothered with gradual steps. You can either come down by the staircase or you can jump from the terrace. It depends on you. Listen to your nature.

There are a few persons who will not bother to come by the staircase, who are not ready to wait even for that. Once they hear the call, they jump. Once the call has been heard, they cannot wait for a single moment. But these are rare people.

When I am saying 'rare,' I don't mean in any evaluatory way. I am not evaluating. I am not saying 'higher'. When I say 'rare', it is just a statement of fact; these people are not many. I am not saying—don't miss my point—I am not saying that they are higher than ordinary people. Nobody is higher and nobody is lower—but people are different. There are people who would like to jump. They should choose Zen. There are people who would like to get to the goal with ease, with cautiousness, with gradual steps. Perfectly good. Go gracefully, if that is your way.

Always remember, it is you, your type, your nature, which has to be the deciding factor. Don't follow Patanjali or Zen. Always listen to your being. Patanjalis and Zen exist for you; you don't exist for them. The sabbath is for man—not vice versa. All religions exist for you, not vice versa. Ultimately, you are the goal.

✆

> *When I listen to my feelings, my inner voice,*
> *they tell me to do nothing, just to sleep, eat, and*
> *play on the beach. I am afraid to follow these*
> *feelings because I think I will get too weak to*
> *survive in this world. Will existence protect me*
> *when I allow myself to let go?*

First thing: there is no need to survive in *this* world. This world is a madhouse. There is no need to survive in it. There is no need to survive in the world of ambition, politics, ego. It is the disease. But there is another way to be, and the whole religious standpoint is: that you can be in this world and not be of it.

When I listen to my feelings and inner voice, they tell me to do nothing . . . Then don't do anything. There is nobody higher than you, and God speaks to you directly. Start trusting your inner feelings. Then don't do anything. If you feel just to sleep, eat, and play on the beach, perfect. Let that be your religion. Don't be afraid then.

You will have to drop fear. And if it is a question of choosing between the inner feeling and fear, choose the inner feeling. Don't choose fear. So many people have chosen their religion out of fear, so they live in a limbo. They are neither religious nor worldly. They live in indecision.

Fear is not going to help. Fear always means the fear of the unknown. Fear always means the fear of death. Fear always means the fear of being lost, but if you really want to be alive, you have to accept the possibility of being lost. You have to accept the insecurity of the unknown, the discomfort and the inconvenience of the unfamiliar, the strange. That is the price one has to pay for the blessing that follows it, and nothing can be achieved without paying for it. You have to pay for it: otherwise you will remain fear-paralyzed. Your whole life will be lost.

Enjoy whatsoever your inner feeling is.

I think that I will get too weak to survive in this world. There is no need. This is fear speaking in you, fear creating more fears. Out of fear more fear is born.

Will existence protect me? Again the fear is asking for guarantees, promises. Who is there to give you a guarantee? Who can be a guarantee for your life? You are asking for some sort of an insurance. No, there is no possibility. In existence, nothing is insured—nothing can be. And it is good. Otherwise, if existence is also insured, you will be already completely dead. Then the whole thrill of it, of being alive like a young leaf in the strong wind, will be lost.

Life is beautiful because it is insecure. Life is beautiful because there is death. Life is beautiful because it can be missed. If you cannot miss it, everything is forced upon you, even life becomes an imprisonment. You will not be able to enjoy it. Even if you are ordered to be blissful, commanded to be free, then bliss and freedom both are gone.

Will existence protect me when I allow myself to let go? Try. Only one thing I can say to you . . . I am not talking to your fear, remember. Only one thing I can say to you all—those who have tried have found that it protects. But I am not talking to your fear. I am simply encouraging your adventure, that's all. I am persuading, seducing you towards adventure. I am not talking to your fear. All those who have tried have found that infinite is the protection.

But I don't know whether you can understand the protection that the universe gives to you. Your protection that you are asking for cannot be given by the universe because you don't know what you are asking. You are asking for death. Only a dead body is absolutely protected. Something alive is always in danger. To be alive is a hazard. More alive—more adventure, more hazard, more danger.

Nietzsche used to have a motto on his wall: live dangerously. Somebody asked him, 'Why have you written this?' He said, 'Just to remind me, because my fear is tremendous.'

Live dangerously because that's the only way to live. There is no other. Always listen to the call of the unknown and be on the move. Never try to become settled anywhere. To be settled is to die: it is a premature death.

I was attending a birthday party, a small girl's birthday, and many toys were there and many presents, and the girl was really happy, and all her friends were there and they were dancing. Suddenly, she asked her mother, 'Mom, were there such beautiful days in the past, when you used to be alive?'

People die before their death. People settle in security, comfort, convenience. People settle in a grave-like existence.

I am not talking to your fear.

Will existence protect me when I allow myself to let go? It has always protected, and I can't think it is just going to be different to you. I cannot believe that it is going to be an exception. It has always been so. It has protected those who have left themselves to it, who have abandoned themselves to it, who have surrendered themselves to it.

Follow nature. Follow your inner nature.

I was reading an anecdote; I liked it very much:

It was spring on the Columbia University campus, and

KEEP OFF signs sprang up on the freshly seeded lawns. The students ignored the warnings, which were followed by special requests, and continued tramping across the grass. The issue became rather heated, until finally the buildings and grounds officials took the problem to General Eisenhower, at that time, president of the university.

'Did you ever notice,' asked Eisenhower, 'how much quicker it is to head directly where you are going? Why not find out which route the students are going to take anyway and build the walks there?'

This is how life should be. The roads, the walks, the principles should not be fixed beforehand.

Allow yourself a let-go. Flow naturally and let that be your way. Walk, and by walking, make your way. Don't follow superhighways. They are dead, and you are not going to find anything on them. Everything has already been removed. If you follow a superway, you are moving away from nature. Nature knows no ways, no fixed patterns. It flows in a thousand and one patterns, but all spontaneous. Go and watch . . . sit on the beach and watch the sea. Millions of waves arising, but each wave unique and different. You cannot find two waves similar. They don't follow any pattern. No man worth the name will follow any pattern.

People come to me and they say, 'Show us the way.' I tell them, 'Don't ask that.' I can only tell you how to walk—I cannot show you the way. Please try to see the distinction: I can only tell you how to walk, and how to walk courageously. I cannot show you the way, because the way is for cowards. Those who don't know how to walk, paralyzed, for them the way exists. For those who know how to walk, they go into the wilderness, and just by walking, they create their way.

And each one reaches to God in a different way. You cannot reach as a mass and you cannot reach as a crowd. You reach alone, absolutely alone.

God is wild. He's not yet civilized—and I hope that he will never be civilized. He is still spontaneous, and he loves spontaneity. So if your inner nature says to go to the beach and to relax, do that. That is from where your God is calling you.

I teach you just to be yourself, nothing else. It is very difficult to understand me because out of your fear, you would like me to give you a pattern of life, a discipline, a style, a way of life.

Persons like me have always been misunderstood. A Lao Tzu, a Zarathustra, an Epicurus, have always been misunderstood. The most religious people were thought to be irreligious because if someone is really religious, he will teach you freedom, he will teach you love. He will not teach you law; he will teach you love. He will not teach you a dead pattern of life. He will teach you chaos, an anarchy, because stars are born only out of chaos. He will teach you how to be totally free.

I know there is fear, there is fear of freedom; otherwise why should there be so many prisons all around the world? Why should people carry prisons around their life continuously—invisible prisons? There are only two types of prisoners I have come across: a few who live in a visible prison, and the remaining who live in an invisible prison. They carry their prison around themselves—in the name of conscience, in the name of morality, in the name of tradition, in the name of this and that.

Thousands are the names of bondage and slavery. Freedom has no name. There are not many types of freedom: freedom is one. Have you ever watched? Truth is one. Lies can be millions. You can lie in million ways: you cannot say the truth in million ways. Truth is simple: one way is enough. Love is one: laws are millions. Freedom is one: prisons are many.

And unless you are very alert, you will never be able to move freely. At the most, you can change prisons. From one prison you can go to the other prison, and you can enjoy the walk between the two. That's what is happening in the world. A Catholic becomes a Communist, a Hindu becomes a Christian, a Mohammedan becomes a Hindu, and they enjoy—yes, there is a little freedom felt just when they are changing the prisons: from one prison to another— the walk in between. They feel good.

Again they are in the same trap in a different name.

All ideologies are prisons. I teach you to beware of them—my ideology included.

✆

A few times recently I have felt that I could fly,
felt curiously exonerated from gravity and looked
with boredom on the 150 pounds' truth of my
body, is this just craziness . . .?

No. You are a meeting place of two dimensions. One dimension belongs to the earth: the dimension of gravity, which pulls you down—that 150 pounds truth of your body. Another dimension belongs to grace, the dimension of God, the dimension of freedom, in which you can go on rising high and high and high and there is no weight in it.

Meditating, this will happen. Many times in deep

meditation, you will suddenly become aware as if the gravitation has disappeared, that now nothing holds you down, that it is now up to you to decide whether to fly or not, that now it is up to you—if you want, you can simply fly into the sky . . . and the whole sky is yours. But when you will open the eyes, suddenly, the body is there, the earth is there, the gravitation is there. When you were with closed eyes, meditating, you forgot your body. You moved in a different dimension, the dimension of grace.

These two things have to be understood: gravitation is the law which pulls you down; grace is the law which pulls you up. Science has not yet discovered, maybe it is not going to discover it ever, the other law. It has discovered one law. You have heard the story—it happened or not, that is not the point—that Newton was sitting in a garden, and one apple fell. Watching that apple fall, Newton started thinking, 'Why does the apple fall towards the earth? Why directly towards the earth? Why not sideways? Why does it not start flying upwards?' The law of gravitation was discovered, that the earth has a pull and pulls everything towards it.

But Newton saw the fruit falling; he didn't see the tree rising up. That's where I have always . . . Whenever I read the story, I always felt he saw the small fruit falling towards the earth; he didn't see the tree rising upwards. You throw a stone. It falls back, true, but a tree goes on rising higher and higher. Something pulling the tree up. A stone is dead; the tree is alive. Life goes higher and higher and higher.

Man, in his consciousness, has reached the highest point on this earth. When you close your eyes to the world, when you are in a deep meditative mood, prayerful, blissful, ecstatic—suddenly, the body is not there. You have become aware of the inner tree of life, and it is going higher and higher, and suddenly you feel that you can fly.

Nothing is crazy in it, but please don't try it. Don't jump out of the window and don't start flying. Then it will be crazy. A few people under LSD or marijuana have done that. Nobody has ever done it under meditation. That's the beauty of meditation, and that is the danger of drugs. A few people under the impression, under a deep hypnotic impression of some chemical drug, have become aware of this grace, that they can fly. The body is forgotten—and they *have* tried. One girl in New York really did it. From the fortieth storey of a building, she simply flew out of the window—then Newton starts working. Then you are the tree no more: you become the fruit. Then you fall to the earth and you crash.

That is one of the dangers of drugs, because they can reveal to you certain truths—but you are not aware. You can commit something, you can do something which can be dangerous. But never has it happened in meditation, because meditation gives you two things together: it gives you a new dimension and it gives you more awareness, so you know it is there, but you are also aware that the body is there. You are still spread in two dimensions.

One day, a very fat, stout gentleman was discussing his tennis technique, 'My brain tells me, run forward speedily, start right away, slam the ball gracefully over the net.'

I asked him, 'And then what happens?'

He said, 'And then?' The fellow became very sad and said, 'My body says, "Who, me?"'

Remember, you are both the body and the consciousness.

You are spread in both dimensions. You are the meeting point of the earth and the sky, of grace and gravity. Nothing is crazy in it. It is simply the truth.

And sometimes it is possible, because it has happened, and it is better I should make you aware of it, sometimes it is possible that actually your body rises a little higher. There is a woman in Bavaria who rises four feet high while meditating. She has been put under scientific observation and has been found not to be deceiving in any way. She remains for a few minutes, four, five minutes, hanging in the air, four feet high. This is one of the oldest experiences of yogis. Rarely it happens, but sometimes it has happened in the past. Sometimes it also happens now. Sometimes it can happen to some of you.

If the pull of the grace becomes too much and the balance is lost, it happens. It is not a very good thing. Don't try, and don't ask for it. It is an imbalance, and it is dangerous for life. When the pull of the grace becomes too much and the pull of the gravity is less, it happens, the body can rise high. Even then, don't think yourself crazy, and don't start feeling that something like insanity is happening to you.

Newton is not all truth. There are greater truths than Newton. And gravitation is not the only dimension; there are many more dimensions.

Man is an infinity, and we have started believing only in part of it. So whenever anything from another dimension enters, we start feeling that something is going wrong. In fact, in the West, many people who are thought to be mad, neurotic, psychotic, and who are in the mad asylums, in mad hospitals, are not really mad. Many of them have had some glimpses of the unknown, but society does not accept that unknown, does not recognize it. Immediately, whenever a person has some glimpse of the unknown, he's thought to be crazy, because he becomes somebody strange. We cannot believe him.

There are books written on Jesus in which it is said that he was a neurotic because he used to hear God and his voice. There are books written about Mohammed that he was mad, he must have heard the Koran in delirium—because who is there to talk to you?—and he heard God speaking, and God said, 'Write!' and he started writing. Because it is not your experience, it is a natural tendency of the mind to say that he must have gone in some madness, must be in delirium, must have been in high fever, because such things happen only when you are not in your senses.

Yes, these things happen in madness also, and these things happen in supersanity also, in superconsciousness also. Because the mad person falls below the normal level of consciousness, he loses control of his mind. Losing control of one's mind, one becomes available to the unknown forces. A yogi, a mystic, achieves to *sanyama*, control of his consciousness. He rises high and goes beyond the normal—again, the unknown becomes available to him. But the difference is that the madman is a victim of the unknown, and the mystic is a master of the unknown. Both start talking in the same way, and you can misunderstand. You can get confused.

Don't think yourself crazy. It is perfectly okay. But don't try it. Enjoy it, allow it; because once you start thinking that it is crazy, you will stop it; and that stopping will disturb your meditation. Enjoy it, as in a dream you fly. Close your eyes; in meditation go wherever you want.

Rise higher and higher into the sky, and many more things soon will become available to you—and don't be afraid. It is the greatest adventure—greater than going to the moon. Becoming an astronaut of the inner space is the greatest adventure.

ॐ

You told me to be myself. I don't understand.
How can I be myself if I don't know myself?

Whether you know or not, you cannot be other than yourself. To be yourself, knowledge is not needed. A rose bush is a rose bush. Not that the rose bush knows that it is a rose bush. A rock is a rock. Not that the rock knows that it is a rock. Knowledge is not needed. In fact, it is because of knowledge that you are missing to be yourself.

You ask, 'You told me to be myself. I don't understand. How can I be myself if I don't know myself?' Knowledge is creating the problem. Look at the rose bush. It is not confused. Every day it goes on being a rose bush. Not even for a single day does it become confused. It does not start some morning growing marigolds; it goes on being a rose bush. It is not confused at all.

Knowledge is not needed for being. In fact, you are missing your being because of knowledge. Unnecessarily, knowledge creates a problem.

I was reading about a certain man named Dudley.

To celebrate Uncle Dudley's seventy-fifth birthday, an aviation enthusiast offered to take him for a plane ride over the little West Virginia town where he had spent all his life. Uncle Dudley accepted the offer.

Back on the ground, after circling over the town for

twenty minutes, his friend asked, 'Were you scared, Uncle Dudley?'

'No,' was the hesitant answer, 'but I never did put my full weight down.'

In an airplane, whether you put your full weight down or not, the weight is carried by the airplane.

Whether you know yourself or not is not the point. Knowledge is disturbing you. Just think, if there was also a rock on that airplane with Uncle Dudley, the rock would have put the whole weight down. And do you think Uncle Dudley can do something, can help in some way? Is there any possibility that he will not be able to put his whole weight on the airplane? He is putting the whole weight, but he is unnecessarily worried. He could have rested, he could have relaxed just like the rock, but the rock has no knowledge and Uncle Dudley has knowledge.

The whole problem of humanity is that humanity knows, and because of knowing, the being is unnecessarily forgotten.

Meditation is how to drop knowledge. Meditation means how to become ignorant again. Meditation means how to become a child again, a rose bush, a rock. Meditation means how just to be and not to think.

When I say to you to be yourself, I mean meditate. Don't try to be anybody else. You cannot be! You can try, and you can deceive yourself and you can promise yourself and you can hope that some day you will become somebody else, but you cannot become. These are only illusions that you can go on having. These are dreams. They are not going to become realities ever. You will remain yourself whatsoever you do.

Why not relax? Uncle Dudley, put your full weight on the airplane. Relax.

In relaxation, suddenly, you will start enjoying your being, and the effort to be somebody else will stop. That is your worry, how to be somebody else, how to be like somebody else, how to become like a buddha, how to become like Patanjali. You can only be yourself. Accept it, rejoice in it, delight in it. Relax.

Zen masters say to their disciples, 'Beware of Buddha. If you meet him on the way, kill him immediately.' What do they mean? They mean there is a human tendency to become imitators. In the English language, there is a book, *Imitation of Christ*. Never before and never after was such an ugly title given to any book. Imitation? But, in a way, that title is very symbolic. It shows the whole mind of humanity. People are trying to imitate, to become somebody else.

Nobody can become a Christ and, in fact, there is no need—God will be bored if you become Christ. He wants somebody new, something original. He wants you, and he wants you to be just yourself.

ॐ

> When you talk of taking the jump, I feel that I
> want to take the jump, but I also feel that I am
> not at the edge from which the jump is taken.
> I see you shaking us but cannot feel it. How do
> I come to the edge? How can I let you teach
> me?

Everybody is always on the edge because each moment, if you dare, the jump is possible. Each moment gives you the edge; and when you ask how to come to the edge, you are being clever. Don't try to be clever. Your question is a trick so you can console yourself that you are not a coward because the edge is not there, so 'from where to take the jump?' So, first the edge has to be found—and it will never be found, because it is right in front of you. Wherever you are standing, you are always at the sharp edge from where you can take the jump. And you ask a very clever question: that first teach me how to find the edge.

Just look in front of you. Just look. Wherever you are that doesn't matter.

And you say, 'I see you shaking us but I cannot feel it.' The problem is not that you are asleep. If you are asleep, it is easy to shake you up out of your sleep. You are pretending that you are asleep; then it becomes impossible. You can see that I am shaking, but nothing is happening. How can you see if you are asleep?

Let me tell you one anecdote. It happened one summer afternoon. The father had promised the children to go for a walk, and he didn't want it. For months he was waiting for this day to rest, so he played, he pretended, that he is fast asleep.

The father played possum while his youngsters tried their best to rouse him from a Sunday afternoon nap to take them for a promised walk, but in vain. They did all sorts of things to wake him. They shook him, they shouted at him, but to no avail. All efforts failed. They even became afraid, what has happened? And the father was pretending to be asleep. Finally, his four-year-old daughter pried open one of his eyelids, peered carefully, then reported, 'He is still in there.'

And I know you are also in there.

And you also know that you are pretending.

It is up to you. You can prolong the game as far as you like, because it is at *your* cost. I am not worried by it. If you want to pretend, okay. Perfectly okay. Do it. But I can see . . . I can see all of you pretending to be asleep—afraid of getting up, afraid of realizing your being, afraid to move.

Just see the truth of it. Don't ask about ways how you can find the edge. You are standing on it.

Don't try to be clever, because in the inner world to be clever is to be stupid. In the inner world, to be stupid is to be clever. In the inner world, those who are ignorant achieve faster than those who are knowledgeable. In the inner world, those who are innocent—and ignorance is innocence . . . Ignorance is beautiful; ignorance is tremendously beautiful and innocent.

Just realize what I am saying! I know you are listening. I can peer into your eyes: I can open your eyelids. I have been doing so every day, and I can see you are still in there. You are not dead, you are not asleep. You are pretending that you are asleep.

And whenever—it is up to you—whenever you decide not to pretend, I am there to help you. I cannot push you against yourself. That is not allowed. God does not allow it, because it gives you total freedom; and total freedom includes everything—to go astray, to fall asleep, to commit sin, to deny God, to commit suicide, to destroy yourself. Total freedom includes all. And God loves freedom, because God is freedom.

❧

Osho, the computer has collected too many of your words. But your smile—it cannot comprehend it.

This is half of the question. The other half I will read later on. First, I should answer the first half.

The late French President Renee Coty attending an abstract art exhibit in Paris was asked if he understood the pictures. With a sigh he said, 'It has taken me all my life to understand that it is not necessary to understand everything.'

The second half:

Will you just be silent with us and smile?

You will not be able to see it. The smile that you can see will not be my smile, and the smile that is mine, you will not be able to see it. The silence that you can understand will not be my silence, and the silence that is mine, you will not be able to understand it, because you can understand only that which you have tasted already.

I can smile—in fact, I am smiling all the time—but if it is my smile, you cannot see it. When I smile in your way, then you understand; but then there is no point.

I am silent all the way, all the time. Even while I am speaking, I am silent because speaking does not disturb my silence. If by speaking the silence is disturbed, it is not worth. My silence is big enough. It can contain words, it can contain speaking. My silence is big enough, it is not disturbed by anything. My silence is not afraid of words.

You have seen people who are silent, then they don't speak. Their silence seems to be *against* speech—and a silence which is against speech is still part of speech. It is absence; it is not presence.

Absence of speech is not my silence! My silence is a presence. It can speak to you, it can sing to you. My silence has tremendous energy. It is not a vacuum; it is a fulfilment.

ॐ

5. Piling Up the Zeros of Being

11. *Samadhi Parinam, the inner transformation, is the gradual settling of distractions and the simultaneous rising of one-pointedness.*

12. *Ekagrata Parinam, one-pointed transformation, is the condition of the mind in which the object of the mind that is subsiding is replaced in the next moment by an exactly similar object.*

13. *By what has been said in the last four sutras, the property, character, and condition, transformations in the elements and sense organs are also explained.*

14. *Whether they be latent, active, or unmanifest, all properties inhere in the substratum.*

THE STORY IS told of Leo Tolstoy, the great Russian novelist, that he was walking in a forest one day when he came upon a clearing and saw a lizard sitting upon a rock, sunning itself. Tolstoy began speaking to the lizard, 'Your heart is beating,' he said. 'The sun is shining; you are happy.' And after a pause, he added, 'But I am not.'

Why are lizards happy and man is not? Why is the whole creation in a celebration and man is not? Why, except man, is everything beautifully tuned unto itself and tuned with the whole? Why is man an exception? What has happened to man? What misfortune has fallen to him? This has to be understood as deeply as possible because from that very understanding starts the path, from that very understanding you become a seeker, from that very understanding you are no longer part of the human disease. You start transcending it.

A lizard exists in the present. A lizard has no idea of the past, no idea of the future. A lizard is just here-now, sunning itself. This moment is enough unto a lizard, but this moment is not enough unto a man and there arises the disease because whenever you will get, you will get only one moment. You will never get two moments together. And wherever you are, you will always be here: and whenever you become aware, you will become aware in the now. The past is no more, the future not yet—and we go on missing that which is for that future which is not yet, for that past which is no more.

To be a lizard on a rock sunning is to be a meditator. Drop the past, drop the future. What does it mean? It means drop thinking because all thoughts either belong to the past or to the future. There is no thought here-now. Thinking has no present tense about it—either it is dead or unborn. It is always unreal—either part of memory or part of imagination. It is never real. The real is never a thought:

the real is an experience. The real is an existential experience.

You can dance in the real, you can sun yourself in the real, you can sing in the real, you can love in the real: but you cannot think it—because thinking is always *about* it, and in that 'about' is hidden the whole misery. In that 'about' you go on moving—about and about—and you never come to the point that was always and always available.

The whole point of all meditation is to be a lizard, sunning yourself on a rock, to be here-now, to be part of the whole, not trying to jump ahead in the future, not trying to carry that which is no more. Unburdened of the past, unconcerned with the future, how can you be miserable? How can Leo Tolstoy be miserable unburdened by the past, unconcerned with the future? Where can misery exist? Where can it hide itself? Suddenly, you explode into a totally different dimension; you go beyond time and you become part of eternity.

But we go on and on like a stuck gramophone record, repeating ourselves endlessly.

I have heard . . .

Two girls were talking in the park and one of them looked so glum, so sad, that the other was feeling very sympathetic. She put her arms around the mink coat of the other gorgeous doll and said, 'Angeline, what is troubling you?'

Angeline shrugged and said, 'Oh, it is nothing, I suppose, but a fortnight ago, old Mr Short dropped dead. You remember him? He was always so good to me. Anyway, he dropped dead and left me Rs 50,000. Then, last week, poor old Mr Pilkinhouse had a seizure and died and left me Rs 60,000. And this week, nothing.'

This is the trouble—always expecting, always asking for more, for more. And there can be no end for this demand for more. Whatsoever you get, you can always imagine more and you can always become miserable.

Poor people are miserable, you can understand, but rich people are also miserable. Those who have are as much miserable as those who have not. Ill people are miserable, but healthy are also miserable. Misery seems to be somewhere else. Misery does not disappear by wealth, health, or anything of that sort. It continues like an undercurrent.

Misery exists in the demand for more, and the human mind can always imagine for more. Can you imagine a situation in which you cannot imagine for more? Impossible. Even heaven can be improved upon. Nobody can imagine a situation in which imagination can stop and you cannot imagine more and a better situation. That means you will be miserable wherever you are. Even heaven won't be enough, so don't wait for heaven. If you go right now into heaven, it won't be enough. You will be as miserable as here. Maybe even more because here, at least, you can hope—that heaven is there and one day or other you will enter into it. If you enter into it, even that hope is gone.

As you are, you can only be in hell, because hell or heaven are ways of looking at things. They are not physical spaces: they are attitudes how you look at things.

A lizard is in heaven and Leo Tolstoy is in hell. Even a man like Leo Tolstoy. He was world-famous, more fame you cannot imagine. His name is going to be in the history books. His books will be read forever and forever. He was a genius. But you cannot imagine a more miserable man. He was rich, one of the richest men in Russia. He belonged to the royal family; he was a prince, married to a very beautiful princess; but you cannot imagine a more miserable man, who was continuously thinking of suicide. He started thinking maybe it is because he is so rich, that's why he is miserable, so he started living like a poor man, like a peasant; but still the misery continued.

What was troubling him? He was a man of great imagination—a novelist has to be. He was a man of tremendous imagination, so whatsoever was available, was always less. More he could imagine, better he could imagine. That became his misery.

Remember this, that if you are expecting anything from life, you will not get anything. Don't expect and it is there in all its glory. Don't expect, don't ask, and it showers upon you in all its miraculousness. All its magic is there. Just wait a little while without thoughts . . . but that seems to be impossible.

Not that there are not moments when you are without thoughts. Patanjali says there are. All those who have entered into the inner space of man, they know there are gaps. But you are missing them somehow, because those gaps are in the present. You jump from one thought to another, and in between was the gap. In between was the heaven—you jump from one hell to another.

In between is heaven, but in between you are not. From one thought to another thought you jump. Each thought feeds your ego, helps you to be, defines you, gives you a boundary, a shape, a form, an identity. You don't look in the gap between the two thoughts because to look into that gap is to look into your original face, which has no identity. To look into that gap is to look into eternity, where you are going to be lost.

You have become so afraid of looking into the gap that you have almost managed to forget them.

Between two thoughts there is a gap, but you don't see it. You see one thought, then you see another thought, then another thought . . . Just watch a little. The thoughts are not overlapping. Each thought is separate. In between the two there must be a gap. There is a gap, and that interval is the door. From that door, you will enter into existence again. From that door, you have been expelled from the garden of Eden. From that door, you will enter into the garden of Eden again, you will again become like a lizard sunning on a rock.

I have heard . . .

Once a family moved from the country to the city, and his mother gave little Bobby careful instructions about traffic. 'Never cross the street until the cars have passed,' she said as he started off to visit a little friend. About an hour later he returned, his eyes brimming with tears. 'What has happened?' his mother asked in alarm.

'I could not go,' said Bobby. 'I waited and waited, but a car never did come by.'

He was told to wait until the cars have passed by, but never a car did come by. The road was empty, and he was looking for cars.

This is the situation inside you. The road is always empty—available—but you are looking for cars, thoughts, and then you become very much worried. So many thoughts.

They become multiplied, they echo and re-echo in you, and you go on being attentive towards them. Your gestalt is wrong.

Change the gestalt. If you look into the thoughts, you create a mind in yourself. If you look into the gaps, you create meditation into yourself. The accumulation of the gaps is meditation; the accumulation of thoughts is the mind. These are two gestalts, two possibilities of your being; either you be through the mind, or you be through the meditation.

Look for the gaps. They are already there, naturally available. Meditation is not something which has to be produced by effort. It is there as much as the mind. In fact, more than the mind because mind is only on the surface, the waves, and the meditation is the depth of the ocean.

Every moment God is seeking you as much as you are seeking him. You may not be seeking him consciously. You may be seeking him under different names. You may be seeking him as bliss. You may be seeking him as happiness, joy. You may be seeking him as forgetfulness, absorption. You may be seeking him as music, as love. You may be seeking him in different ways, under different names. Those names do not matter: you are seeking him—knowingly, unknowingly. And one thing you have to understand, he is also seeking you. Because unless the search is from both the sides, the meeting is not possible.

The whole is seeking the part as much as the part is seeking the whole. The flower is seeking the sun as much as the sun is seeking the flower. The lizard is not only sunning, the sun is also *lizarding*. It is a connected whole. It has to be so, otherwise things will fall apart. It is one piece, it is one harmony, it is one dance. All gestures, all movements, are connected together. They have to be; otherwise they will fall apart and the existence will no longer be existence—it will disappear.

Let me tell you through a parable. Consider the following parable:

Man, let us say, is climbing a mountain—because in the valley he has lived and in the valley he has dreamed and in the valley he has thought and imagined, but there has only been frustration. In the valley he has remained empty, unfulfilled, so he thinks that at the top of the mountain is God. Valley he has lived. The top remains far away; shining in the sun it remains an attraction. The far away always calls you, invites you. To look at the close is very difficult; not to look at the far away is also very difficult. To be interested in that which is close is very difficult; to be not interested in that which is very far is also very difficult. The far away has a tremendous attraction, and the top of the mountain goes on calling you.

And, when you start feeling empty in the valley, of course, it is logical to think that the one you are seeking does not live in the valley. He must be living at the top. It is natural for the mind to move from one extreme to the other, from the valley to the peak.

At the top of the mountain, man thinks is God, down in the valley are the cares and concerns of human life, all the troubles of love and war. In the valley you go on gathering anxiety, in the valley you go on gathering dust, in the valley, by and by, you become dull and dead. The valley looks like a graveyard. One wants to get out of it. One starts thinking of freedom, *moksha*, of how to get out of the imprisonment the valley has become—how to get out of attachment, love; how to get out of ambition, violence, war; how to get out of society, the very society which gives you the opportunity to be worried, in fact, forces you towards anxiety and anguish.

One starts thinking, but this is an escape. In fact, you are not going to the peak; you are going away from the valley. It is not that the peak has called you. In fact, it is the valley which is pushing you. You are still pushed by the valley; and pushed by the valley, you can never be free. It is not that you are going on your own. You are being expelled. The valley is creating a situation in which you cannot live there anymore. Life becomes too much. A moment comes to everybody's life when it becomes too much, the world is too much, and one starts escaping.

Man starts escaping towards the peak. And now comes the most important part of the parable: God, on the other hand, is coming down the mountain. Because, let us say, He is fed up with His purity and aloneness.

Man is fed up with the crowd, with the impurity; God is fed up with His aloneness and purity.

Have you ever watched? You can be happy alone very easily. To be happy with somebody else becomes very difficult. One person can be happy very easily, very cheaply, there is no cost to it. Two persons together, it becomes very difficult to be happy. It is easy to be unhappy now—without any cost, very cheaply. And if three persons are together, it is impossible to be happy—at no cost is happiness possible.

Man is fed up with the crowd, nowhere to move, nowhere where you can find a space of your own, always onlookers and onlookers—you are always on the stage, always performing—and the eyes of the crowd watching you. No privacy. By and by, one gets fed up, bored.

But God is also bored. He is alone, pure, but purity itself becomes boring when it remains and remains and remains.

God is coming down towards the valley; His desire is to plunge into the world. Man's desire is to jump out of the world, and God's desire is to plunge into the world. Man's desire is to be God, and God's desire is to be man.

There is a truth of withdrawal and there is a truth of return. Man is always withdrawing, and God is always returning. Otherwise, the creation would have stopped long ago, if God was not returning continuously. It must be a circle. The Ganges goes on falling into the ocean, and the ocean goes on rising into the clouds and goes on falling on the Himalayas—back to the Ganges, and the Ganges goes on flowing. The Ganges is always withdrawing, and the ocean is always returning. Man always seeking God, God always seeking man; this is the whole complete circle. If only man was going towards God and God was not coming, the world would have stopped long ago. It would have stopped anytime because one day all men will return and God will not be coming back; the world will disappear.

But the peak cannot exist without the valley; and God cannot exist without the world; and day cannot exist without night; and life is impossible to conceive of without death.

It is very difficult to understand this, that God is a constant returning, man a constant withdrawal—man a constant renunciation, sanyas, and God a constant coming back to the world, a celebration.

There is a truth of withdrawal and there is a truth of

return. Separately, they are both half and partial: together, they become *the* truth, the whole truth.

Religion is a withdrawal, but then it is half. Religion should also be a return, then it is whole. Religion should teach you how to go into yourself and religion should also teach you how to come back again because somewhere in between the valley and the peak God and man meet. If you bypass God . . . And there is every possibility because if you are going up the hill and He is coming down the hill, you won't even look at Him. There may even be condemnation in your eyes. How can this be God who is going back to the valley? You may even look at Him with the eyes of 'holier than you'.

Remember this: whenever God will meet you, you will see Him coming back to the world; and you are leaving the world. That's why your so-called mahatmas, your so-called saints, never come to understand what God is. They go on talking about a dead concept of God, but they never know what God is because they will always miss. Somewhere on the path, you will meet Him, but your sense won't even look at Him. He will look like a sinner; He is going back to the world.

But if they reach to the top, they will find it empty. The world is too full; the top is too empty. They will not even find God there, because He is always returning. He is always coming, He is always creating. He is never finished. The creation is an endless process. God is not an entity. He is a process, the process of returning.

If you can meet Him on the way and you can recognize Him, only then is there a possibility. Then you will drop the idea of going to the peak . . . you will start returning. All great ones who have understood, first have gone into withdrawal, and then they have returned to the world, back in the marketplace with all their meditation in a tremendous flowering. But they have come back to the world. They have understood the point. They have understood the point of wholeness, of holiness. They have understood the point that the outer and the inner are not two and the creation and the creator are not two and matter and mind are not two—that the sacred and the profane are not two. They are one. All duality has disappeared for them. This is what I call *advait*, non-duality—the real message of Vedanta, the real message of yoga.

It is very natural to get fed up with the world. It is very natural to seek freedom, nothing special in it.

It happened:

Mulla Nasruddin was celebrating his twenty-fifth wedding anniversary, and he gave a big party for all his friends. He invited me, too. But the host was nowhere to be seen. Finally, I found him in the library drinking brandy and staring into the fire.

'Mulla,' I said, 'you should be celebrating with your guests. Why are you sad and what are you doing here!'

'Why am I so sad?' He explained, 'When I had been married for five years, I had decided to kill my wife. I went to my lawyer and told him what I was going to do. He said if I did it, I would get twenty years in prison. Just think,' said Mulla to me, 'tonight, I would have been a free man.'

It is very natural. The world is too troublesome. It creates so much anxiety: it creates so many imprisonments. To seek freedom, to inquire about it, is natural—nothing special in it. It becomes special when you have understood, when you come from the peak back to the valley with a new dance in your step, with a new song on your lips, with a totally new being—when you come absolutely pure into the world of impurity, unafraid because now you are incorruptible.

When you come back to the prison on your own accord, voluntarily, when you come to the prison as a free man and you accept the prison, back to your cell; now it is a prison no more because freedom cannot be imprisoned. Only a slave can be imprisoned. A free man cannot be imprisoned—he can live in the prison, and free. And unless your freedom is that powerful, it is not worth.

Now the sutras.

Samadhi is a word very difficult to translate into English; there exists no parallel. But in Greek there is a word which is parallel; that word is *ataraxia*. The Greek word means quiet, calm, of deep inner contentment. That is the meaning of *samadhi*: so contented, so deeply contented, that nothing disturbs now, nothing distracts now. So deeply in tune with existence, in a sort of atonement—at-one-ment—that now there is no problem. There is no other who can disturb; the other has disappeared. The other disappears with your thoughts. The thought is the other. In the gaps is the *samadhi*, *ataraxia*. In the gaps is calm and quiet.

Not that when you have attained to it, you will not be able to think, no. Not that your capacity to think will disappear. In fact, just on the contrary, when you live in the gap, you become capable of thinking for the first time. Before it, you were just victims, victims of a social atmosphere, victims of a thousand and one thoughts surrounding you—not a single thought of your own. They were thoughts; you were not capable of thinking. Those thoughts had settled on you as birds settle on a tree by the evening. They had entered in you. They were not original; they were all borrowed.

You had been living a life which is a borrowed life. That's why you were sad. That's why there was no life in you. That's why you looked dead, there was no vibration. That's why there was no joy, no delight. Everything was blocked by borrowed thoughts. Your whole stream was blocked. You could not flow because of borrowed thoughts. When you become a part of *samadhi*, *ataraxia*, a deep inner calm of the gaps, intervals; you become, for the first time, capable of seeing, of thinking—but now these thoughts will be your own. Now you will be able to create an original thought. You will be able to live an original life, fresh, fresh as the morning, fresh as the morning breeze. You will become creative.

In *samadhi*, you become a creator because in *samadhi*, you become part of God.

There is a saying of Pascal's that most of man's troubles come from his not being able to sit quietly in his chamber. Yes, that is true. If you can sit quietly in your inner chamber, almost all the troubles will disappear. You create them by running hither and thither. You create them by unnecessarily getting attached to your thoughts—which are not yours. You create them because you cannot sit at rest.

ॐ

Samadhi Parinam, the inner transformation, is the gradual settling of distractions and the simultaneous rising of one-pointedness.

First Patanjali talked about *nirodh parinam*, to look into the gap between two thoughts. If you go on looking, slowly thoughts settle, distractions settle—slowly, as if somebody has passed, bullock carts have passed from a mountain stream, and because of the passing wheels and the people, much dust has risen up towards the surface. The whole stream, which was just a few seconds before so crystal clear, is now absolutely dirty, muddled. But then the bullock carts have gone and the people have gone and the stream goes on flowing: by and by, as time passes, again the dust settles back to the bed, again the stream becomes crystal clear.

When you look into the gaps, the bullock carts, the crowd of your thoughts which has disturbed your being so completely, by and by goes away, far away, and your inner stream of consciousness starts settling. This is what Patanjali calls *samadhi parinam*, the inner transformation '. . . is the gradual settling of distractions and the simultaneous rising of one-pointedness'. It has two parts to it. On the one hand, distractions settle, and on the other hand, one-pointedness arises.

When you are full of thoughts too much, you are not one man. You are not one consciousness; you are almost a crowd, a multitude. When there are thoughts and your gestalt is to look at thoughts, you are divided; you are divided in as many parts as there are thoughts to your mind. Each thought becomes a division of your being. You become polypsychic; you are not uni-psychic. You are not one, you become many, because each thought carries a part of you and divides you—and those thoughts are running in all directions. You are almost mad.

I have heard:

An old Scottish guide returned from taking the new minister on a grouse shooting trip over the moors and sank wearily into his chair before the fire.

'Here is a cup of hot tea for you, Angus,' said his wife. 'And is the new minister a good shot?'

The old fellow puffed his pipe a bit, then he replied, 'Ah, a fine shot he is, but it is marvellous, indeed, how the Lord protects the birds when he is shooting.'

You have been missing your target because you are not one-pointed. You have been missing all that you wanted because you are not one-pointed. The whole misery of man is that he is running in many directions simultaneously—absolutely undecided, indecisive, not knowing where he is going, not knowing what he is doing.

I have heard that two politicians met at a psychoanalyst's door. One was coming out, and the other, who was getting in, asked, 'Are you coming in, or are you going out?' The one who was coming out said, 'Well, if I did know whether I am coming out or coming in, I would not have been here.'

Nobody knows whether one is coming out or coming in. Where are you going? What are you seeking?

You go on missing because your target goes on changing. It is a flux. There are a thousand and one targets around you, and you are a thousand and one, a crowd—a crowd shooting at a crowd of targets. The whole life proves to be empty.

Samadhi parinam, the inner transformation, is the gradual settling of distractions and the simultaneous rising of one-pointedness. As thoughts disappear—thoughts are distractions—one-pointedness arises. You become one. The stream of consciousness flows in a direction, it becomes directed. It has a direction now. It can reach; it can become a fulfilment.

✄

Ekagrata parinam, one-pointed transformation,
is the condition of the mind in which the object
of the mind that is subsiding is replaced in the
next moment by an exactly similar object.

Ordinarily, one thought goes, another comes of a totally different character. Sadness goes/happiness comes. Happiness goes/frustration comes. Frustration goes/anger comes. Anger goes/sadness comes. The climate around you goes on changing, and with the climate, you. Every moment you have a different colour to your being. Hence, no wonder that you don't know who you are—because in the morning you were angry, by lunchtime you were happy, in the afternoon, you were sad, by the evening, you were frustrated. You don't know who you are. You change so much because each colour that passes you becomes your identity for a few moments.

Ekagrata parinam is a state of your consciousness where this change stops. You become one-pointed. And not only that, if you want to retain one state of affairs, you become capable of retaining it. If you want to remain happy, happiness is replaced by happiness, again by happiness, again by happiness. If you want to remain happy, you remain happy. If you want to remain sad, it is up to you. But then, you are the master. Otherwise, everything goes on changing.

I go on observing you. It seems almost unbelievable how you manage. One day a couple comes to me and they say, 'We are in deep love. Bless us.' And the next day, they are back and they say, 'We have been fighting, and we have separated.' Which is true? The love, or the fight? Nothing seems to be true with you. Everything seems to be just a flux. Nothing seems to stay. Nothing seems to be a part of your being. Everything seems to be just a part of your thinking process—with one thought, one colour; with another thought, another colour.

It happened:

A near-sighted girl, too vain to wear glasses, was determined to get married. She finally found herself a husband and went off to honeymoon at Niagara Falls with him. When she returned, her mother gave a shriek, ran to the telephone and called an oculist.

'Doctor,' she gasped, 'you have got to come over here right away. It is an emergency. My daughter has always refused to wear glasses, and now she is back from her honeymoon, and . . .'

'Madam,' interrupted the doctor, 'please control yourself. Have your daughter come to my office. No matter how bad her eyes are, it can't possibly be that much of an emergency.'

'Oh no?' said the mother. 'Well, this fellow she has got with her is not the same one she left for Niagara Falls.'

But this is the situation of everybody. The man you love in the morning, you hate in the evening. The man you hate in the morning, you fall in love with by the evening. The man or the woman who looked beautiful just the other day, today has become ugly.

And it is an emergency case.

And this way you go on, like a driftwood, just at the mercy of the winds. The wind changes its course, and your course is changed. You don't have any soul yet.

Gurdjieff used to say to his disciples, 'First *be*, because right now you are not. Let this be your only goal in life—to *be*.' Somebody will ask him, 'How can we love?' He will say, 'Don't ask nonsense. First be, because unless you are, how can you love?'

Unless you are, how can you be happy? Unless you are, how can you do something? The being is needed in the first place, then everything becomes possible.

Jesus says, 'Seek first ye the kingdom of God, and then all shall be added unto you.' I would like to change it a little: Seek first ye the being, the kingdom of being, and then all shall be added unto you. And that is the meaning of Jesus. The kingdom of God is an old term for the kingdom of being. First be, then everything is possible, but right now when I look into you, you are not there. Many guests are there, but the host is missing.

Ekagrata parinam, one-pointedness in consciousness is a basic necessity so that your being can arise. In a flux, the being will not be possible. At the most, you can go on becoming this and that and that, but you will never be a being.

✆

> *By what has been said in the last four sutras,*
> *the property, character and condition,*
> *transformations in the elements and sense organs*
> *are also explained.*

And Patanjali says, this is the situation: the world is

changing around you, the body is changing, the senses are changing, the mind is changing—everything is changing—and if you are also changing, there is no possibility of finding the eternal, the unchanging one. These are changing, that is true. The world is changing continuously. It is a process: it has no being. It is a flux. Let it be so. There is only one thing permanent in the world, and that is change. Everything else changes—except change. Only change remains as a permanent character.

The body is changing, continuously, every moment. Every single moment it is flowing and changing; otherwise, how will you become old, how will you become a youth, how will a child become a youth? Can you say on what day the child becomes a youth? Can you say on what date the young man becomes old? Difficult. In fact, if you ask physiologists, they are not yet clear at exactly what moment one says that the man was alive and now he is dead. It is impossible to decide. The definition is still unclear because life is a process. In fact, when you have died, almost, and your friends have abandoned you, a few processes still continue in the body—nails go on growing, hair go on growing. A part of you still seems to be alive and functioning.

When exactly a man dies, it is still undefined. In fact, life and death cannot be defined; it is a flux phenomenon. Body goes on changing, mind goes on changing—every moment the mind is changing.

If you are looking into this changing world in these distractions of your being, and searching for truth, God, bliss, you will be frustrated. Move within. Go into the gaps where neither the world exists nor the body nor the mind. There, for the first time, you come face to face with eternity, which has no beginning and no end, which has no change in it.

∅

Whether they be latent, active, or unmanifest,
all properties inhere in the substratum.

Patanjali says whether a flower has died or whether a flower is in bloom makes no difference. When a flower is in bloom, he is dying, and when a flower has died, he is again trying to come back up. Creation goes on through a process of uncreation and creation, uncreation and creation. This is what Patanjali calls *prakriti*. *Prakriti*, again, is a word which cannot be translated. It is not only creation: it is the very process of creation and uncreation.

Everything becomes manifest, disappears, becomes unmanifest: but it remains in the substratum, the *prakriti*. Again, it will come back. Summer comes and then goes: again, the summer is back, coming. Winter is there, going: again, it will come. It goes on moving. Flowers appear, disappear. Clouds come, disappear. The world goes on moving in a cycle.

Things have two states: manifest and unmanifest. You are beyond them. You are neither manifest nor unmanifest. You are the witness. Through *nirodh parinam*, through the gap between two thoughts, you will have the first glimpse of it. Then go on gathering those gaps, go on piling up those gaps. And always remember, whenever two gaps are there, they become one. Two gaps cannot be two. They are not like two things; they are two emptinesses. They cannot be two. You bring two zeros near, they become one. They jump into each other because two zeros cannot be *two* zeros. Zero is always one. You bring a thousand and one zeros home—they will jump into each other and become one.

So go on piling up those gaps, zeros of being and, by and by, what Patanjali first calls *nirodh* becomes *samadhi*. In *samadhi*, distractions disappear, go distant and distant and distant . . . and then disappear; and one-pointedness arises in your being. That is the first glimpse of who you are beyond *prakriti*, beyond this game of creation and uncreation, beyond this game of waves and no waves, flowers and no flowers, of change, movement, momentariness. You become a witness.

That witness is your being.

And to attain that is the whole goal of yoga.

Yoga means: *Unio Mystica*. It means the union, the mystic union with oneself. And if you are one with yourself, suddenly you realize you have become one with the whole, with God, because when you move into your being, it is an emptiness again, a silence, a tremendous non-ending silence . . . and God is also silence. Two silences cannot be two— they jump into each other and become one.

You withdraw into yourself, and God is returning. You meet on the way: you become one. This oneness is the meaning of the word 'yoga'. Yoga means to become one.

ॐ

6. You Can't Get There From Here

Why do I always ask nearly the same questions, again and again?

BECAUSE THE MIND itself is repetition. The mind is never original. It cannot be; by its nature it is such. The mind is a borrowed thing. It is never new; it is always old. Mind means the past—it is always out of date. And, by and by, mind becomes a pattern, a habit, a mechanism. Then you become very efficient in it. Then you go on moving in the same rut, in the same routine, again and again and again.

You go on asking the same questions because you go on remaining the same mind.

Unless you are new, your questions are not going to be new. Unless you drop the old mind completely, totally, utterly, the new question cannot get into you. The new question cannot get into you because there is no space, you are already filled by the old. And the mind has a persistent habit of repeating itself; it is more efficient. The mind is very stubborn. Even if it pretends to change, the change is not real, just a pretension, a modified form of the old. Maybe the language changes, the form changes, but the deep question remains the same . . . and the mind goes on persisting.

You have to see it. This question is good. At least, this question is not old.

This is from Saroj. She has been asking questions, and I have been never answering her, but today I decided to answer because this is a new glimpse, that she has understood one thing; that she has been asking again and again the same old thing. This understanding is new. A new morning, a new dawn has come to her mind. Her consciousness has become alert to a certain old pattern.

Help this awareness; cooperate with it. By and by, you will start seeing yourself in two dimensions: the dimension of the mind—the old, the past; and the dimension of consciousness—always fresh and always new, always original.

I will tell you one anecdote:

A man excitedly ran up to another man on the street and slapped him heartily on the back. 'Paul Porter,' he greeted him, 'am I glad to see you! But tell me, Paul, what in the world happened to you? Last time I saw you, you were short and fat. All of a sudden you seem tall and thin.'

'Look, sir,' the puzzled man answered, 'I am not Paul Porter.'

'Ah!' boomed the undaunted greeter, contemptuously, 'Changed your name too, eh?'

The mind has a persistent habit to go on believing in itself—even against all facts. Even if your old mind goes on giving you nothing but misery and hell, you go on believing in it.

People say that this is an age of unbelief. I don't see it. The same old belief in the mind continues. Somebody is a Hindu; he believes in Hinduism because his mind has been conditioned to be a Hindu. Somebody is a Christian; he believes in Christianity because his mind has been conditioned to be a Christian. Somebody is a communist; he goes on believing in communism because his mind has been conditioned to be a communist. All the three are one. They are not different people. They may have different names and labels, but the same thing is happening to all of them; they are all conditioned and clinging to the mind and they all believe in the mind.

I call that man religious who renounces the mind. I call that man religious who renounces all conditionings, who stops clinging to the mind, who starts moving into consciousness, who becomes more and more aware of the conditionings. And in that very awareness, one becomes loose of the conditions—and that is the only freedom there is. All else is just rubbish. All talk of freedom—political, economic, social—is just rubbish. There is only one freedom, and that freedom is freedom from conditionings, freedom from the mind, becoming alert, aware, attentive, and moving in a new dimension.

Good, Saroj, that you have become aware that your questions have been repetitively the same. That's why I was not answering them. It is useless because when the mind goes on persisting in its old habit, it doesn't listen.

Try always to find the new, the fresh, the young—that which is just being born. Catch that before it becomes old, dissolve into it before it becomes a pattern. Never make your life a patterned and structured thing. Let it remain a flow, unfrozen, fluid, moving always into the unknown.

Mind means the known. And you are the unknown. If you understand this, you will use the mind, and you will never be used by the mind.

ॐ

There are many who can see a lot of contradictions in what you are saying. Once you explained why this is so. But up to this moment I have not come across one single contradiction. Even when there obviously should be one. I just cannot see it, even when I try to. Is there anything wrong with me? Please explain.

No, nothing is wrong with you. The wrong is with others who keep on seeing contradictions, but they are in the majority. You will be alone. So don't be overpowered by the majority. Don't be dominated by the majority. Remain alone. Truth is never of the crowd; it is always of the individual. Truth is never of the many; it is always of the few, of the rare. It is not of the multitude, it is of the unique. This difference has to be understood.

The scientific truth is not unique. The scientific truth, in fact, debars the unique. It only listens to the repetitive. Science goes on saying that unless an experiment can be repeated, it cannot be believed. When an experiment can be repeated a thousand and one times and it always gives the same result, then it gathers evidence of being true.

Religious truth is of the unique. A Buddha cannot be repeated, a Jesus cannot be repeated. They come once and then they disappear. They come as if out of the blue, and then they disappear again into emptiness—and there is no way to repeat them. That's why science goes on denying them because science believes only in something which can become a mechanical repetition. If Buddha can be produced on order—if Buddha can be produced like Ford cars, on an assembly line, then science can believe. But that is not possible.

Religion is the realm of the unique, of the rare, of that which cannot be repeated, of the unrepeatable; and science is the realm of the repeatable. That's why science remains part of the mind and religion goes beyond mind, because all that can be repeated, mind can understand.

People see contradictions in me because I don't repeat. They see contradictions in me because their mind has been trained in a certain Aristotelian logic. The Aristotelian logic says that either this is white or black. If it is white, it cannot be black; if it is black, it cannot be white. The Aristotelian logic teaches you; either this or that. That is the base of all scientific mind. The religious mind says it is both; white is also black, and black is also white. It cannot be otherwise because religion sees so deeply that opposites become one there.

Life must also be death, and death life, because somewhere the religious mind, religious consciousness comes to understand that they are meeting—already they are meeting in you. Something is dying, something is being born. Each moment I see you dying, each moment I see you reborn. You are not a continuity. Each moment something dissolves, each moment something new comes into existence. But you are not aware, so you cannot see the gap. Because you cannot see the gap, it looks like a continuity.

Religion believes that there are no contradictions— there cannot be—because existence is one. Religion believes and sees that there is no polarity. Even if there is a polarity, it is not polar and opposite, it is complementary, because existence is non-dual; it is one. Life cannot be separate from death, and night cannot be separate from day, and summer cannot be separate from winter, and old age cannot be separate from childhood.

Childhood grows into old age, night changes into day, day changes into night. No and yes are not a question of either/or; they are both together. Two points on one line— maybe on the extreme ends, but the line is one. So whenever a religious person exists, he cannot be consistent in the same way as a scientist is. He has a deeper consistency. It is not apparent on the surface; it is deep in his being.

I am not a philosopher and I am not trying to prove any theory to you, and I am not here talking to you to prove some hypothesis. There is nothing to prove. Truth is there, already given. Religion has nothing to prove; it has no theory about it. It simply gives you a way how to see that which is already there. I go on talking to you, not that I have a theory. If I have a theory, I will be consistent. I will always look whether it fits with my theory or not; if it fits, okay; if it doesn't fit, I drop it. But I have no theory.

Everything fits with me. If I have a theory, I have to look at my theory. Then the fact becomes secondary and the theory becomes primary. If the fact fits with the theory, it is okay; if it doesn't fit, I have to ignore it.

I have no theory. Every fact, just by being a fact, fits with me, fits with me perfectly. Only very few will become aware of it. So don't be worried. If others see contradictions, they have an Aristotelian conditioning.

My whole effort is to help you melt so your structure dissolves and, by and by, you can start seeing opposites as complementaries. If you love me—this will happen immediately because the heart knows no contradictions. Even if there is a contradiction on the surface, the heart knows somewhere deep down there must be a consistency; this contradiction must be meeting somewhere. It must be held together by something which goes beyond the contradiction.

I am a unity. If you watch me, if you love me, you will be able to see the unity. Once you see my unity, then whatsoever I say comes out of that unity. It has to be consistent. Whether rationally you can understand or not, that is not the point. The heart has its own reasons, and those reasons are deeper than the reasons of reason.

When people listen to me, people who are not in any way committed to me, people who are not in any way deeply related to me, people who are not travelling with me into the unknown, then whatsoever I say, they understand it in their own way—they interpret it. Then it is not the thing that I have said. Something else has entered into it; their interpretation. And because of their interpretation, the whole colour changes, the purity is lost, and then there are problems. Those problems are of their own making.

I have heard a story:

Patrick went to confession and told the priest, 'Father, I love my neighbour.'

The priest said, 'That's wonderful. I am glad to see that your attendance at services in this church has benefited you and taught you the ways of the Lord. Carry on the good work. That is the whole message of Jesus: Love your neighbour as thyself.'

Patrick went home, changed into some more comfortable dress, and slipped next door. He rang the bell and said, 'Is it all right?'

The lady said, 'Well, Albert is out, but this is afternoon and broad daylight. Someone might see you coming here.'

'It is all right,' said Patrick. 'I have got a special dispensation from Father O'Brien.'

Love thy neighbour as thyself. When Jesus says it, he means something totally different. When Patrick interprets it, it becomes totally different. 'Love thy neighbour,' is a prayer, it is a meditation, it is a whole way of being, but when ordinary mind listens to it, it takes a different colour. Love becomes sex. Prayer becomes infatuation. And the mind is very cunning; it goes on taking any support—whatsoever is available from anywhere—for its own ends.

When you listen to me, beware. You may be interpreting me in your own way. When I say 'freedom', you may interpret it as 'license'. Watch. When I say 'love', you may interpret it as 'sex'. Watch. Look at your interpretations because they are the traps—and then you will find many contradictions in me because I am there no more; now it is you reflected. You have many contradictions in you. You are almost a confusion. You have many minds in you, and you go on interpreting in many ways, and then you see contradictions—in your own interpretations.

Listen to me. Even more than listening—be with me. Then all contradictions disappear.

ॐ

The third question is a beautiful story from Devateertha:

*Your story, Osho, about Uncle Dudley reminds
me of another West Virginia story. So it goes
that a stranger to the area was searching for a
certain place. He got lost, so he stopped to ask
an old farmer for direction.*

*The old man replied, 'Go three miles north,
over the bridge, make a right, go six miles
ahead to a broken-down barn, turn left at the
Hickory fence . . . Nope. That won't do it.'*

*Again he tried, 'Follow this here road for four
miles, over the creek, around the bend by the
chestnut tree, make a right, follow that road
about two miles, turn left by the stop sign . . .
Nope wrong again.'*

*Trying once more, the old man said, 'Head
West till you hit Gruber's General Store, follow
to the right over the bridge for five miles, turn
right by the yellow house. Go over three ridges
till you come to a fork in the road, bear right
. . . Nope. That won't do.' 'So,' said the old
farmer after serious contemplation, 'You can't
get there from here.'*

I have always loved that story. It is tremendously significant.
Let me repeat the last part. He said, 'Sorry, you can't get
there from here.'

In fact, from here, you can get only to here. From here,
there is no way to there. From here, always you can get to
here—from here to here is the only possibility. From here,
there is no way to there. From now, you get to now—again
and again—because it is always present. From today, you
never get to tomorrow. Remember, from today you come

back to today again and again and again—because there is no tomorrow. Today remains; it is an eternity. Now is an eternity, and here is the only space.

The man may have been drunk, but sometimes drunkards utter tremendously meaningful truths. Why? Because drunkards can never remain in the Aristotelian logic. That may be the appeal of alcohol, of drugs; it relaxes you. Your head which is divided by Aristotle— between here and there, between now and then, between today and tomorrow—that division disappears. You settle deeply in you. You regain your lost childhood when everything was everything else and everything was meeting and merging into everything else, and there were no boundaries.

Watch a child. When he gets up in the morning, sometimes he may be crying because he has lost a toy in the dream. In fact, there is no boundary between dream and day—there is no boundary between dream and reality. Everything meets and merges into each other. A child lives in a totally different world—the world which is one, the world of the mystics, the world of the non-dualists, *advaitins*, the world where there are no distinctions, where things are not divided against each other.

That old man may have been drunk that day. Otherwise, when you are in your senses, you cannot say such a thing. He tried hard. He tried hard to catch hold of his Aristotelian mind. He tried hard to get into the old categories which have become dim under alcohol and its influence. He tried hard to find a way but again and again he got lost. Finally, he said it is not possible, 'Sorry, you cannot get there from here!'

This conclusion of the anecdote would be loved by Zen

masters. They will see the point, because they are also drunkards—drunk with God. Again the same happens; categories disappear, distinctions disappear. Says Lao Tzu, 'Everybody is clear-headed, only I am muddled.' Lao Tzu and muddled? Says Lao Tzu, 'Everybody knows what is what, only I don't know. Everybody is wise, only I am ignorant.' The very word 'Lao Tzu' means either 'the old fellow' or 'the old idiot'. Maybe enemies were calling him Lao Tzu and meaning the old idiot, and friends were calling him Lao Tzu, meaning the old fellow; but he was both.

Remember, there is nowhere to go. You carry your here and now around you. Wherever you go, it is always here; wherever you go, it is always now. Here and now are the eternities, and they are not two. In language, we have become accustomed to calling them two, because in language, Einstein has still to be introduced. Einstein has proved it now as a scientific fact that space and time are not two. He has coined a new word 'spatio-time' to make them one. If that is right, here and now cannot be two. 'Here-now' is the word of the future. Sooner or later, when Einstein is absorbed into languages, these words will lose distinction. Here-now.

The story is beautiful. Sometimes in small anecdotes, in folklore, in stories of the people, much wisdom is hidden. Don't just laugh at them. Sometimes through your laughing, you may be trying to escape from something which can make you uncomfortable. Nobody writes these stories; they grow like trees. Through centuries, a thousand and one minds work on them. They go on changing and being refined continuously. They are a part of human heritage. Whenever a joke is told, don't just laugh and forget it.

Laugh, perfectly true and right, absolutely okay, but don't miss the joke in the laughter. It may have something of tremendous value hidden in it. If you can see it, your own consciousness will be enriched.

ॐ

Recently, I had a glimpse of emptiness. In my work, I communicate through images juxtaposed strangely. Will the clearing process allow the image to rise anew, or as I vanish, will the work vanish?

It depends. If your work is just a profession, it can vanish when you vanish. When your ego disappears into deep meditation, your profession can also disappear, but if it is not a profession but a vocation, if it is not just a job but a calling, if it is not just imposed on you by yourself or by others but has deeper sources within you, deeper springs to feed it and nourish it, then when the ego disappears, your work for the first time becomes your love; then you become more creative. Tremendous energy is released when the ego disappears because the ego is carrying much of your energy—wasting much of your energy. Just watch for twenty-four hours. Your ego is taking so much energy—in anger, in pride, in trips. So much energy is wasted. When the ego disappears, all that energy becomes available to your work, to you.

It can become creative, but then the creativity has a very different quality, a different taste and savour. Then it is not as if you are creating; it is as if you have become a vehicle, as if you are possessed by something greater than you, as if existence has made you an instrument, a medium. You have become a flute and now God sings. You are just a hollow, a passage; you allow the whole to flow through you. If there is any fault, it is yours. If there is any beauty, it is God's. If you err, you err. If something is really given birth through you, you feel grateful. Then all mistakes are yours because then you must have hindered in some way. Blocked, you must not have been totally empty. The passage was not clear for God to flow through. But whenever something beautiful happens—a painting, a poetry, a dance, or whatsoever—you feel deeply grateful. A prayer comes to your heart; a thankfulness comes to your heart.

Then your creativity has a very quiet, calm quality to it. Right now, with the ego, there is much turmoil and tumult. With the ego, the creativity is nothing much but the noise that you are a creator. The poetry may not be worth, but the poet goes on shouting from the housetops. The painting may not be of any value, may not have anything original to it, may be just an imitation, a fake; but the painter goes on carrying his head high in pride. It is very noisy with the ego. When the ego disappears, you flow in many ways, but everything becomes very silent and quiet.

I have heard:

Someone once asked Professor Charles Townsend Copeland of Harvard why he lived on the top floor of Hollis Hall in his small, dusty old rooms. 'I shall always live here,' he answered. 'It is the only place in Cambridge where God alone is above me.' Then, after a pause, he said, 'He is busy, but he is quiet.'

Yes, God is busy, tremendously busy—spread all over existence. Just see how many things he is doing together, simultaneously. This infinite expanse is his. You must have seen pictures of Hindu gods with thousands of hands. They are very symbolic. They show that he cannot work with two hands. Two hands won't be enough. The work is so vast. You must have seen Hindu gods with three heads looking in three directions—because if he has only one head, what will happen to his back? He has to look in all directions. He has to be busy everywhere, with a thousand and one hands . . . but so quiet—not even claiming, 'I have done so much.'

And you do a small thing—you just arrange a few words and you think it is a poem—and now arises the pride and you go mad. And you start claiming that you have created something. Remember, only mediocres claim. The real creators never claim, because the real creators become so humble, they understand that it is none of their own. In fact, they have only been vehicles.

When Rabindranath, a great poet, used to have moods, was possessed, he would go in a room, close his door. For a few days he will not eat, he will not come out. He will just silently listen to the voice of God. He will purify himself so that he can become the right vehicle. He will cry and weep and he will go on writing. And whenever anybody asked, he would always say, 'Whatsoever is beautiful is not mine, and whatsoever is ordinary must be mine. I must have added it.'

When Coleridge died, almost 40,000 incomplete pieces of poetry and stories were found—40,000. Almost all his life his friends were saying, 'Why don't you complete them?' He said, 'How can I complete? He starts; he has to complete—whenever he wills. I am helpless. One day he possessed me and then a few lines came—and only one line is missing, but I am not going to add it because that will become destructive to it. Seven lines from the sky and one line from the earth? No, it will cut the wings. I will wait. If he is not in a hurry, who am I to worry about it?' This is a real creator.

A real creator is not a creator at all. A real creator becomes instrumental; he is possessed of the great forces. Wild forces of God possess him, wild seas and skies of God possess him. He becomes a mouthpiece. He utters, but the words are not his. He paints, but the colours are not his. He sings, but the sounds are not his. He dances, but he dances as if possessed—somebody else dancing through him.

So it depends. The question is, if your ego disappears into meditation, what will happen to your work? If it is a profession, it will disappear, and it is good that it disappears. Nobody should be a professional. Your work should be your love; otherwise the work becomes destructive. Then somehow you drag it and your whole life becomes dull. Your whole life becomes empty in a negative sense, unfulfilled. You are doing something which you never wanted to do in the first place. It is violent. It is suicidal—you are killing yourself slowly, poisoning your own system. Nobody should be a professional. Your work should be your love; it should be your prayer. It should be your religion, not your profession.

There should be a passion flowing between you and your work. When you have really found your vocation, it is a love affair. It is not that you have to do it. It is not that you have to force yourself to do it. Suddenly, you do it in a totally different way which you had not known before. Your steps have a difference dance, your heart goes on humming. Your whole system functions for the first time at the optimum. It is a fulfilment. Through it you will find your being—it will become a mirror; it will reflect you. Whatsoever it is—a small thing.

It is not a question that only great things become vocations, no. A small thing. You may be making toys for children, or making shoes, or weaving cloth—or whatsoever.

It doesn't matter what it is, but if you love it, if you have fallen in love with it; if you are flowing with no reservation, if you are not withholding yourself, if you are not dragging—dancingly moving into it—it will cleanse you, it will purify you. Your thinking, by and by, will disappear. It will be a silent music and, by and by, you will feel that it is not only work, it is your being. Each step fulfilled, something in you flowers.

And richest is the man who has found his vocation. And richest is the man who starts feeling a fulfilment through his work. Then the whole life becomes a worship.

Work should be a worship, but that's possible only when your being starts to be more meditative. Through meditation, you will gather courage. Through meditation, you will gather courage to throw the profession and to move towards the vocation.

Maybe through the profession, you could have been rich, but that richness would have been of the outside.

Through the vocation, you may remain poor; you may not be so rich. Society may not pay for it because society has its own ends.

You may be writing poetry and nobody may be purchasing them because society does not need poetry. It can afford—it is foolish enough—it can afford to be without poetry. It pays if you are preparing something for war, for violence. If you are doing something for love—a poetry is something for love, people will be more loving—society doesn't bother. Society needs soldiers, society needs bombs, society needs weapons not worship.

The society may not pay you, you may remain poor, but I tell you that poverty, that risk, is worth taking because inner riches will be overflowing towards you. You may die poor as far as your outside is concerned, but you will die an emperor as far as your inner being is concerned—and ultimately only that is of any value.

ᛤ

My body is extraordinarily ill—rogi. My mind is scientifically indulgent—bhogi. My heart is approximately yogi. Nearing to child's totality of action, non-politicalness, innocent and truthloving, are there any chances of enlightenment for me in this life? Guide me and expedite my case for the kingdom of God. Prepared for the worst, I hope for the best.

The body is helpful if it is healthy, but it is not an absolute condition—helpful, but not absolutely necessary. If you can drop the identity with the body, if you start feeling that you are not the body, it doesn't matter whether the body is ill or healthy. If you start going beyond it, transcending it, becoming a witness to it, even in an ill body, enlightenment is possible.

I am not saying that you should all go and become ill. If you are ill, don't feel desperate, don't feel hopeless. A healthy body is helpful. It is easier to go beyond a healthy body than beyond an ill body because the ill body needs attention. It is difficult to forget an ill body. It constantly reminds you of its misery and pain and illness. It constantly calls you back to it. It needs care; it needs attention. It is difficult to forget it—and if you cannot forget it, it is difficult to go beyond it. But difficult—I don't say impossible.

So don't be worried by it. If you feel it is ill, chronically ill, and there is no way to make it healthy, forget about it. You will have to make a little more effort, a little extra effort, to gain witnessing, but it can be gained.

Mohammed was not very healthy. Buddha was constantly ill; he had to always carry a physician with him. Jeevak was the name of the physician who constantly had to attend to Buddha. Shankara died when he was thirty-three; that shows the body was not in very good condition; otherwise he would have lived a little longer. Thirty-three is not the time to die. So don't be worried; don't make it a hindrance.

Secondly, you say, *My mind is scientifically indulgent— bhogi.* If it is really scientifically indulgent, you can come out of it. Only an unscientific mind can go on repeating the stupidity of indulgence. If you are really a little alert, scientifically observant, sooner or later you will come out of it—because how can you go on repeating?

For example, sex. Nothing bad in it, but to go on repeating it for your whole life shows that you are a little stupid. I don't say there is some sin in it—no. It simply shows that you are a little stupid. The religions have been telling you that sex is sin. I don't say so. It is simply foolishness. Allowed, nothing wrong in it, but if you are intelligent, you will come out of it—one day or the other. Greater the intelligence, sooner the day will come when you will understand that, 'Yes, it's okay. It has a time, it has a meaning at a certain stage of life, but then one comes out of it.' It is a little childish.

Let me tell you a story:

Two elderly people were appearing in court, suing for divorce. The man was ninety-two and the woman was eighty-four. The judge spoke first to the man, 'How old are you?'

'Ninety-two, Your Honour.'

Then he spoke to the woman.

'I am eighty-four,' she admitted shyly.

Said the judge to the man, 'How long have you two been married?'

'Sixty-seven years,' grimaced the old-timer.

'And you mean you actually want to terminate a marriage that has lasted almost seventy years?' demanded the judge unbelievingly.

The old man shrugged and said, 'Look, Your Honour, whichever way you look at it, enough is enough.'

Whichever way you look at it . . . If you are intelligent, you will not wait for ninety-two years—enough is enough will come sooner. The more intelligent you are, the sooner it will come. Buddha left the world of indulgence when he was just young. His first child was born, and the first child was only one month old when he left. Enough is enough came to him too early. He was really a very, very intelligent man. The more intelligence is there, the sooner the point of transcendence.

So if you think you are really scientific, it is time—old-timer—to understand enough is enough.

And you say, 'My heart is approximately yogi.'

Approximately? That is not the language of the heart. Approximately is the language of the mind. The heart knows only totality—this way or that. Either all or none—the heart does not know anything like approximately. Just go to a woman and tell her, 'I love you approximately.' Then you will know.

How can you love approximately? What does it mean, in fact? That you don't love.

No, the heart still doesn't seem to function. You may have heard a rumour from the heart, but you have not understood it. The heart is always total. For or against does not matter, but it is always total. The heart knows no division; all divisions are of the mind.

The body is ill, there is no problem. A little more effort, that's all. The mind is in indulgence, there is also not much problem. Sooner or later you will understand and come out of it. But the real problem comes with the third; approximately won't do. So look again, deep in your heart. As deep as you can, watch.

Allow the heart to say and whisper to you. If the heart really loves yoga—yoga means the search, the effort to find out what is the truth of life—if really the heart has moved on the search, nothing can prevent it.

Neither indulgence will be a barrier nor illness will be a barrier. The heart can override any situation; the heart is the real source of your energy. Listen to the heart. Trust the heart. And move with the heart. And don't be worried about enlightenment, because that worry is also of the mind. The heart knows nothing about the future; it lives here-now. Search, meditate, love, be here-now; and don't be worried about enlightenment. It comes on its own accord. Who bothers?

If you are ready, it is to come. If you are not ready, thinking constantly about it will not make you ready. In fact, that thinking will function as an obstacle. So forget about enlightenment and don't be worried whether or not it is going to happen in this life.

Whenever you are ready, it will happen. It can happen this moment. It depends on your readiness. Whenever the fruit is ripe, it falls to the ground. Ripeness is all. So don't create unnecessary problems around yourself. Enough. You have illness, that is a problem. Indulgence, that is a problem. Approximate love for yoga and enlightenment, that is a problem. Now no more problems. Please, don't bring this enlightenment in. Forget about it. It has nothing to do with you and your thinking and your expectations, with your hopes or desires. It has nothing to do with them. Whenever you are desireless and ready and the fruit is ripe, it happens on its own accord.

℘

When you die can you make me die too?

I am ready right now to help you. Why wait that long? Why postpone it?

And if you miss me while I am alive, how can you get to me when I am dead? If you cannot flow with me while I am here with you, it will become very, very difficult for you when I am gone. Why postpone?

You are thirsty and I am ready to quench it right now, then why say tomorrow? Why are you afraid? And if you are afraid today, you will be afraid tomorrow. You will be **more** afraid tomorrow because today's fear will have **gathered**. Every day you will go on gathering fear. Drop it.

The very readiness to die is the readiness to be reborn.

I am reminded of a very beautiful story. I would like to share it with you:

Three tortoises, aged 201, 135, and 97, decided to go on a pub crawl in London. They first visited the Star and Garter. A fortnight later, they reached the next pub. Just as they were going in, the oldest one said, 'Oh, dear. I left my wallet back at the other pub.' The youngest of the three said, 'You are too old to go all the way back. I will fetch it for you.' And he went off. Ten days later, just as the two older tortoises reached the bar rail, one of them said, 'Young Arnold has been a heck of a long time fetching your money.' The other said, 'Just like him. He is absolutely unreliable and terribly slow.'

A voice from the doorway suddenly said, 'Damn the pair of you! Just for that, I won't go!'

Don't be that lazy, and don't go on postponing.

ॐ

> *Whenever I am near you, I feel tense and I apparently see three reasons for the same. First: I feel I am being tested and so I have to remain alert. Secondly: I have received so very tremendously from you that in return I would like to give something also and that seems impossible. And thirdly: even so, I feel I still have to receive something from you and I am afraid of missing it.*

It is from Ajit Saraswati, Dr Phadnis. All the three reasons are true, and I am happy that he is alert and aware and can see into things. Yes, all the things are true.

Whenever he is near me, I also feel that he is a little nervous, a little trembling inside. And these are the reasons. And it is good; it is nothing wrong. One has to be that way.

If you start feeling my presence, you can see the gap. Then much has to be bridged. One starts feeling a nervousness, whether it will be possible or not. I am giving you much, and the more you receive, the more you become capable of receiving; and the very possibility that more has to be received creates a nervousness, because it is a responsibility. Growth is a responsibility. It is the greatest responsibility there is . . . and then the fear that may be the opportunity comes and you miss it. And, right, when I give to you, immediately, your heart says give something in return, and that is impossible. That I understand. What can you give . . . except yourself?

All the three causes are true, and it is good that one becomes aware.

ॐ

You have done so much for me. You don't ask that I be better or different. You just keep alleviating the pain and pointing me towards joy. What can I do for you?

It is from Amida. The same question will arise in so many hearts by and by. The question is beautiful, but don't be worried by it. There is no need to do anything for me. Just be. Just be; don't think in terms of doing anything. There is nothing to do, but just by being yourself, you make me tremendously happy. Not that I am not happy already, but just as does a gardener when a new rose bush brings flowers and the garden feels happy, whenever somebody amongst you becomes a being and flowers, I feel tremendously happy.

Just like a painter paints a picture, I work on you. A poet works on a poem, I work on you. You are my poems, my roses, my paintings. Enough that the painting be, nothing else is needed.

❧

Please talk about music and meditation.

They are not two. Music is meditation—meditation crystallized in a certain dimension. Meditation is music—music melting into the dimensionless. They are not two.

If you love music, you love it only because around it somehow you feel meditation happening. You are absorbed by it, you become drunk in it. Something of the unknown starts descending around you . . . God starts whispering. Your heart beats in a different rhythm, one in tune with the universe. Suddenly, you are in a deep orgasm with the whole. A subtle dance enters into your being and doors that have remained closed forever start opening. A new breeze passes through you; dust of the centuries is blown away. You feel as if you have taken a bath, a spiritual bath; you have been under a shower—clean, fresh, virgin.

Music is meditation; meditation is music. These are two doors to approach the same phenomenon.

❧

Watching you sit in your chair, I get more and more puzzled. You are sitting there so incredibly comfortable, you seem to be weightless. What are you doing to the law of gravity?

There is no need to do anything with the law of gravity. Once you become meditative, a different law applies to you; the law of grace. You become available to a different world; the world of grace. Something goes on pulling you upwards. Just as gravitation pulls you downwards, something goes on pulling you upwards. No need to do anything with the law of gravitation. You have just to open a new door into your being from where the law of grace becomes available to you.

✍

7. In a Cold Universe

15. The variation in transformation is caused by the variety in the underlying process.

16. Performing sanyama on the three kinds of transformation—nirodh, samadhi and ekagrata—knowledge of past and future.

17. The sound and the purpose and idea behind it are together in the mind in a confused state. By performing sanyama on the sound, separation happens and there arises comprehension of the meaning of sounds made by any living being.

18. By observing past impressions, knowledge of previous births is obtained.

THERE IS A parable in Friedrich Nietzche's *The Gay Science*. A madman enters a marketplace with a lantern, crying, 'I see God! I see God!' but the busy crowd is unconcerned at his outbursts and laughs at his comical antics. Turning suddenly on them, he demands, 'Whither is God? I shall tell you, we have killed him—you and I.' But as they ignore the enormity of his announcement, he finally flings his lantern to the ground and cries, 'I come too early. My time has not come yet. This tremendous event is still on its way.'

This parable is tremendously significant. As man grows, his God changes. Has to be so because man creates his own God in his own image. It is not vice versa. It is not as it is said in the Bible that God creates man in his own image. Man creates God in his own image. When man's image changes, his God obviously changes. And there comes a point in man's growth when God disappears completely. God as a personal God is out of the immature mind of humanity.

Existence as divine is a totally different concept. Then God is not a personal being somewhere high in the heaven ruling the world, manipulating, controlling, managing. No, all that nonsense disappears as man becomes mature. It is a childhood concept of God, a childish concept of God. If a small child is to understand God, he has to understand as a personal being. When humanity grows and becomes mature, that God is to die. Then a totally different existence arises. Now the whole existence is divine—not that there is God.

For Nietzsche himself, this realization that there is no personal God was too much. He could not bear it: he went insane. He was not ready himself to understand what insight had happened to him. He himself was childish; he needed a personal God. But he meditated upon it, and as he meditated, the more and more he became aware that God is no longer there in the skies. It is dead. And he also became aware that he has been killed by us.

Of course, if it was created by us, it has to be killed by us. The concept was created by man in his childhood. In his maturity the concept is dropped—as when you were children, you played with toys, then you became mature, and you forgot all about those toys. Suddenly, one day you come across in a corner of the house, in the rubbish, an old toy. Then you remember how much you had loved it, but now it is meaningless. It has to be thrown; you have changed.

Man created the personal God, then man destroyed it. This realization was too much for Nietzsche himself; he became insane. His insanity is an indication that he was not prepared for the insight that happened to him.

But, in the East, Patanjali is absolutely godless. You cannot find a greater atheist than Patanjali, but it does not disturb him because, really, he is a grown-up man, really grown-up in consciousness, mature, integrated. For Buddha, God doesn't exist . . .

If there is a personal God, he can forgive Friedrich Nietzsche because he will understand that this man still needed him. That man Nietzsche was still divided, confused—half of his being was saying yes, and half was saying no. If there is a personal God, he can even forgive Gautam Buddha because at least he denied him. He said, 'There is no God.' That too is paying attention. But he will not be able to forgive Patanjali. He used him. He not only denied him, that he is not, he used the very concept as a device. He said, 'For the ultimate growth of man, even the concept of God can be used as a hypothesis.' Patanjali is absolutely cold about God, colder than Gautam Buddha, because when you say no, there is a certain passion, when you say yes, there is a certain passion—in love, in hate, there is passion. Patanjali is absolutely indifferent. He says, 'Yes, the concept of God can be used.' He is the greatest atheist the world has ever known.

But in the West, the concept of atheist is totally different. It is not yet mature. It is on the same plane as the theist is. The theist goes on saying, 'There is a God' in childish terminology, as a father, and the atheist goes on denying, that there is no such God. They both exist on the same plane. Patanjali is the real atheist, but it does not mean that he is irreligious. He is the really religious man. A *really* religious man cannot believe in God. It will look like a paradox.

A really religious man cannot believe in God because to believe in God, he has to divide existence in two—God and no God, the creator and the creation, this world and that, matter and mind. He has to divide, and how can a religious man divide? He does not believe in God; he comes to understand the very divinity of existence. Then the whole existence is divine; then all that is there is divine. Then every place is a temple, and wherever you move and whatsoever you do, you are moving in God and you are doing to God. The total—you included—becomes divine. This has to be understood.

Yoga is a perfect science. It does not teach to believe; it teaches to know. It does not say to you, 'Become blind followers'; it says, 'Open your eyes,' and it gives you the method how to open your eyes. It does not say anything about the truth. It simply says everything about your vision, how to attain the vision, the capacity to see, the eyes, so that whatsoever there is, is revealed to you. It is more than you can ever conceive of; it is more than all your gods put together. It is infinite divineness.

One thing more about this parable. The madman said, 'I come too early. My time has not come yet.' Patanjali came really too early. His time has not come yet. He is still waiting for his time. It always happens that people who realize truth are always ahead of their time—sometimes thousands of years ahead. Patanjali is still ahead of time. Five thousand years have passed; still his time has not come yet. The inner world of man has not yet become a science. He has given all the foundation; he has given the whole structure. The structure is waiting for humanity to come close and to understand it.

Our religions, so-called religions, are juvenile. Patanjali is a giant, a pinnacle of a man. His height is so much that you cannot see the peak; it is hidden somewhere in the clouds. But everything about him is absolutely clear. If you are ready not to cling to your confusion, if you are ready to follow the path that he shows, everything is absolutely clear. About this man Patanjali, there is nothing like mysticism. He is a mathematician of the mystery; he is a logician of the illogical; he is a scientist of the unknown. And it is tremendous even to conceive that one man has put the whole science together. Nothing is lacking, but the science is waiting for humanity to come close so that the science can be understood.

Man understands only that which he wants to understand. His understanding is dominated by his desires. That's why Patanjali, Buddha, Zarathustra, Lao Tzu, they always feel they have come too early. Because man is still asking for toys to play with. He is not ready to grow. He does not want to grow. He clings to stupidities. He has invested too much in his ignorance and he goes on deceiving himself.

Just watch yourself. When you talk about God—you are not talking about God, you are talking about *your*

God. And what sort of God can your God be? It cannot be more than you; it can only be less than you. It cannot be more beautiful than you; it can only be more ugly than you. It cannot be a clarity. It is bound to be a confusion, because in the concept of your God you will be involved. It cannot go higher than you. Your height—at the most—can be the height of your God.

People think according to their desires, ambitions, egos, and everything becomes coloured by it.

It happened that Mulla Nasruddin contested an election.

He received only three votes. His wife, when she came to know, turned to him and snapped, 'There! I always knew you were keeping another woman!'

One vote of Nasruddin, himself, one from his wife, and from where comes the other? The jealous mind thinks in terms of jealousy. The possessive mind thinks in terms of possessiveness. The angry mind thinks in terms of anger.

Look at the Jewish God. He is as possessive as any man can be. He is as egoistic as any man can be. He is as revengeful as any man can be. He does not look divine at all. He looks more like a devil than like a god. The whole myth of Adam being turned out of the garden of Eden shows nothing much about Adam, but it shows much about the God. 'Because Adam disobeyed'—what type of God is that who cannot tolerate such a small disobedience, very intolerant, who cannot tolerate a little freedom? That God may be a slave owner, but he is not a god.

What was the sin of Adam, in fact? Curiosity, nothing else. Because God had said, 'Don't eat the fruit of this tree. This is the tree of knowledge,' and Adam became curious.

Simple, very human. To think otherwise is impossible. And for that small thing—how can you call it a sin? That is the whole base of all scientific curiosity and inquiry. All scientists are sinners. Patanjali, Buddha. Zarathustra—all are sinners because they are tremendously curious to know what truth is, what life is. They are all Adams. But the Jewish God could not tolerate; he became mad. He turned Adam out of the garden; the greatest sin has been committed. Curiosity is a sin? The effort to know the unknown is a sin? Then to seek truth is a sin. Disobeying, being rebellious is a sin? Then all great religious people are sinners because they are all rebellious.

No, it has nothing to do with God. It has something to do with the Jewish mind, small mind thinking about God, creating a God in its own image.

Mulla Nasruddin once staggered from a train, his complexion very white. I had gone to the station to receive him.

'Riding backwards for ten hours,' he explained, 'I never could stand that.'

'Why,' I inquired, 'didn't you ask the person sitting opposite to change seats with you?'

'I could not do that,' said the Mulla. 'There wasn't anybody there.'

There is nobody in the sky to listen to your prayers. Whatsoever you want to do, do. There is nobody who is going to give you permission to do it. Whatsoever you want to be, be. There is nobody you have to look to for permission. Existence is free and available. This is the understanding of yoga: that existence is available to everybody. Whatsoever you want to be, you can be. Everything is ready. Don't wait for anybody's permission because there is nobody. The opposite seat is vacant—if you want to sit, you can sit on it.

Mulla looks absurd, ridiculous, but that's what the whole of humanity has been doing for centuries, looking at the sky, asking permission, praying—to somebody who is not there. Prayer is not the right thing; the right thing is to meditate. And what is the difference? When you pray, you have to believe in someone who is listening to your prayer. When you meditate, you meditate alone. In prayer, the other is required; in meditation, you alone are enough.

Yoga is meditative. It has no place for prayer, because it has no place for God. It has no place for any childish notions about God.

Let this become a constant remembrance, if you really want to be religious, you will have to pass through the state of atheism. If you really want to be authentically religious, don't start by being a theist. Start by being an atheist. Start by being an Adam. Adam is the beginning of Christ. Adam starts the circle and Christ ends the circle. Start by saying 'no' so that your 'yes' can mean something. Don't be afraid and don't believe out of fear. If you have to believe someday, only believe out of knowing and love—never out of fear.

That's why Christianity could not develop a yoga, Judaism could not develop a yoga, Mohammedanism could not develop a yoga. Yoga was developed by people who were courageous enough to say no to all beliefs, to all blind faiths, who were able to deny the convenience of belief to themselves and who were ready to inquire and go into the wildness of their own being.

It is a tremendous responsibility. To be an atheist is to be very deeply responsible because when there is no God, you are left alone in a cold world. When there is no God, you are left alone with nothing to hang on to, with nothing to cling to. Great courage is needed, and you have to create the warmth out of your own being. This is the whole meaning of yoga, to create warmth out of your own being. The existence is cold. No hypothetical God can give you warmth. You are simply dreaming. It may be a wish fulfilment, but it is not true. And it is better to be cold and to remain with truth than to live surrounded by lies and feel warm.

Yoga says, realize the truth that you are alone. You are given an existence; now you have to create meaning out of it. Meaning is not already given.

Existentialists in the West say something with which Patanjali will agree totally. Existentialists say, existence precedes essence. Let me explain it to you.

A rock is there. A rock's essence is given; it is already given. Its existence is its essence also. The rock is not going to grow: it is already that which it can be. But man is different: man is born—he brings his existence, but the essence is not given yet. He comes as an emptiness. Now he has to fill that emptiness by his own effort. He has to create meaning: he has to grope in the dark; he has to work it out, what life means. He has to discover; he has to be creative. Existence is given; essence has to be created—and every moment the way you live, you create your essence. If you don't create it, you will not have it.

People come to me and they ask, 'Please tell us what is the meaning of life.' As if meaning is given somewhere. Meaning is not given, you have to create it.

And this is beautiful. If meaning was already given, man would have been a rock. Then there was no possibility to grow, no possibility to discover, no possibility to adventure—no possibility. In fact, everything closed—a rock is closed from every dimension. It is already that which it can be, but man is not already . . . only a possibility, a trembling possibility, with infinite future, with a thousand and one alternatives. It will depend on you who and what you become.

You are responsible. When there is no God, the responsibility falls totally on you. That's why weaklings go on believing in God. Only very strong men can stand alone. But this is a basic necessity—for yoga this is a basic requirement, that you stand alone and that you come to realize that the meaning is not given; you have to search for it. You have to create it. You will come to a meaning—life can come to a meaning—but that meaning will have to be discovered by your own effort. Whatsoever you do will go on revealing you. Every act will make your life, your existence, more and more meaningful.

Only if this is the truth is yoga then possible. Otherwise, go on praying: otherwise, go on kneeling down on the earth, go on praying to your own ideas and go on interpreting your own prayer, and live in a hallucination, live in an illusion.

Sigmund Freud has written a book. The name of the book is very significant, *The Future of an Illusion*. The book is about religion. It is a misfortune that he never became aware of Patanjali; otherwise he would not have written that book—because religion can exist without illusion. To Sigmund Freud, religion means Christianity and Judaism. He was not aware of the depths of Eastern religions. Western religions are more or less political. Much of them are not religious at all; they are superficial. Eastern religions have gone to the very depth, and this is the depth where you deny God also, and you say now there is no need to depend. Whenever you think you need somebody to depend on, you will create an illusion.

To realize that one is alone in a cold universe—and there is nobody to pray to, and there is nobody to complain to, and there is nobody who is going to help you—only you—it is a tremendous responsibility. One staggers, one feels afraid, one starts trembling. Anguish arises, a great anxiety is created by the very fact that you are left alone.

'God is dead,' Nietzsche said it only a hundred years before; Patanjali knew it 5,000 years before. All those who have come nearer truth have known that God is man's imagination. It is man's interpretation, a lie, to give yourself warmth.

People go on interpreting in their own ways. The whole concern of yoga is that you drop all interpretations, let your eyes be not clouded by any hypothesis and belief, look direct, look unclouded, look without smoke. Let your flame be without smoke and see whatsoever there is.

Overheard in a park: two men were describing their wives to each other. 'Mine is like Venus de Milo.'

'You mean she has a shapely figure and stands about naked?' asked the other.

'No, she is an old relic and she is not all there.'

'Mine makes me think of Mona Lisa.'

'Do you mean she is French and has an enigmatic smile?'

'No, she is as flat as a canvas and she ought to be in a museum.'

People go on interpreting.

Always listen to their meaning, not to their words. Always listen to their innermost being, not the sounds that they make on the outside. What they say is not significant . . . what they are.

Your God, your prayer, is not significant. Your churches, your temples, are not significant. Only you. When you pray, I don't listen to your prayer, I listen to you. When you kneel down on the earth, I don't see your gesture, I see you. It is out of fear—and a religion out of fear is impossible. Religion is possible only out of understanding. That's the effort of Patanjali.

But with Patanjali, also, people go on interpreting. They bring their minds and then Patanjali is there no more. They listen to their own heartbeats in him.

In a small school, the teacher asked a tardy student, 'Why are you late?'

'Well, a sign down the street said . . .'

The teacher, interrupting, 'Now, what can a sign possibly have to do with it?'

'The sign said,' said the student, "School ahead. Go slow.'

It depends on you what you will understand when you read Patanjali. Unless you can leave yourself behind, you will misunderstand. Understanding is possible only when you are absolutely absent—you don't interfere, you don't interrupt, you don't give colours, shapes, and forms. You simply see, with no idea, no prejudice.

ॐ

Now the sutras:

> *The variation in transformation is caused by the variety in the underlying processes.*

You have heard about so many miracles, so many *siddhis*. Patanjali says there is no miracle possible; all miracles follow a certain law. The law may not be known. When the law is not known, people think out of their ignorance that it is a miracle. Patanjali believes in no miracles. He is utterly scientific in his understanding. He says if something happens, there must be a law. The law may not be known, you may be ignorant about it—even the person who is doing the miracle may be unaware of the law, but he has come, stumbled upon how to use it and he is using it.

This is the basic sutra for all miracles. *The variation in transformation is caused by the variety in the underlying processes*. If you change the underlying process, the manifestation changes. You may not be aware of the underlying process; you just see the manifestation. Because you just see the manifestation and you cannot go deep and you cannot see the underlying process, the undercurrent of the basic law, you think there is a miracle. There are no miracles.

For example, alchemists in the West tried hard for centuries to transform base metal into gold. There are reports that a few of them did succeed. Scientists had always been denying it, but now science itself has succeeded in it. Now you cannot deny—now we know the underlying process. Now physics says that the whole world consists of atoms, and atoms consist of electrons. Then what is the difference between gold and steel? The difference is not in the basic reality; both consist of electrons, electric particles. Then what is the difference? Then why are they different? Gold, iron, they are different. And what is the difference? The difference is only in the structure, not in the basic substance.

Sometimes electrons are more, sometimes less—that makes the difference. The quantity makes the difference, but the substance is the same. The structure is different. You can make many types of houses with the same bricks. The bricks are the same. You can make a poor man's hut and you can make a king's palace—the bricks are the same. The basic reality is the same. If you want, the hut can be transformed into a palace and the palace can be transformed into a hut.

This is the basic sutra of Patanjali *The variation in transformation is caused by the variety in the underlying processes.* So if you understand the underlying process, you become capable of things which ordinarily people are not capable of doing.

℘

> *By performing sanyama on the three kinds of transformation—nirodh, samadhi, and ekagrata—knowledge of past and future.*

If you concentrate on *nirodh*, the gaps between two thoughts, and you go on piling up those gaps, you go on accumulating those gaps that is what Patanjali calls *samadhi*—and then arises in you a situation where you become one and one-pointed—*Ekagrata*—if this happens, knowledge of the past and the future.

It will be a miracle if you can know the future. It is not a miracle.

There is a scientific record about a very rare man in the West, Swedenborg. He wrote a letter to Wesley, a famous priest, and told him, 'In the world of the spirits, I have heard the rumour that you want to see me.' Wesley was surprised because he was thinking to see him, but he had not said so to anybody. He could not believe it. He wrote a letter saying, 'I am simply amazed. I don't know what you mean by the world of spirits, I don't know what you mean that you have heard the rumour, but this is certain that I have been thinking to see you—and I have not said this to anybody. I will be coming on such and such date, because I am going for a tour, and three, four months afterwards, I will be coming to you.' Swedenborg wrote to him, 'That is not possible because, exactly on that date, I have heard the rumour in the world of the spirits that I am going to die.' And exactly on that date he died.

Swedenborg was staying with a few friends at a holiday resort, and suddenly he started crying, 'Fire! Fire!' They could not believe what he was saying. They ran out. There was no fire—nothing—it was a small village, a seaside village. They asked him what he meant—and he was perspiring as if there was fire, and he was trembling. Then he said, 'Nearabout three hundred miles away, a town is on fire.' A horseman was sent immediately. He was right. The town was on fire, and at that moment the people of the town became aware, when he said, 'Fire! Fire!'

The queen of Sweden became interested in this man.

She said, 'Can you say something to me which can give me proof that you move in the world of the spirits?' He closed his eyes and he said, 'In your palace,' where he had never been, because he had never been called before to the palace, and it was not a public place where anybody could go . . . He said, 'In a certain room,' the number of the room, 'in a certain drawer, which is locked, and the key will be found in another room, open it. Your husband has left a letter for you'. The husband had been dead for almost twelve years. 'And this is the message on the letter . . .' He wrote the message. The room was found, the key was searched for and found, the drawer was opened, and there was a letter and exactly those were the words that Swedenborg had written on the piece of paper.

Patanjali says if *nirodh* is accomplished, it becomes *samadhi*. If *samadhi* is attained, one becomes one-pointed, consciousness becomes a sword, a sharp, one-pointed thing, knowledge of past and future. Because then for you time disappears and you become part of eternity. Then past is not past for you, and future is not future for you. Then for you, all the three are available simultaneously.

But this is not a miracle. This is a simple law, a basic law. One has to understand and use it.

℘

The sound and the purpose and idea behind it are together in the mind in a confused state. By performing sanyama on the sound, separation happens and there arises comprehension of the meaning of sounds made by any living being.

And Patanjali says, if you bring your *sanyama*—that is your *dharana*, concentration; your contemplation *dhyan*; and your *samadhi*, if you bring all these three—one-pointed—on any sound uttered by any living being, animal, bird—you will understand the meaning of it.

In the West, there are stories about St. Francis that he would talk to animals. He would even talk to donkeys and say, 'Brother donkey.' He would move into the forest and talk to the birds, and birds would come to him. Once, he called from the bank of the river, 'Sisters,' as he used to call the fish, and thousands of fish took their heads up all over the river to listen to him. These are records which have been witnessed by many people.

It is said about Lukman, who created the unani system of medicine, that he would go to the trees and ask their properties, 'For what disease can you be used, sir?' and the tree would answer. In fact, he has reported so many medicines that modern scientists are simply bewildered because methods were not there: experiment was not possible. Only just now are we becoming capable of entering into the hidden properties of things, but Lukman has talked about them.

Patanjali says this too is not a miracle. If you concentrate—you become one and you listen to the sound without any thought—the very sound will reveal to you the truth behind it. It is not a question of understanding the language; it is a question of understanding the silence. If you are in silence, you can understand silence. Ordinarily, if you know English, you can understand English, if you know French, you can understand French. The same is true if you are silent, you can understand silence. That is the language of the whole.

In one-pointedness one becomes absolutely silent. In that absolute silence, everything is revealed—but not a miracle. Patanjali does not like the word 'miracle'. He is a man of science. There is nothing magic-like in it; it is simple.

I was at Mulla Nasruddin's house one day. Mulla Nasruddin and his wife were in the kitchen, washing the dishes. I and Nasruddin's little son, Fajalu, were in the living room, watching television. Suddenly, there was a crash of falling dishes. I and Fajalu listened but heard nothing more.

'It was Mother who dropped them,' little Fajalu announced, finally.

I was amazed. 'How do you know?' I asked him.

'Because she is not saying anything.'

There is a way of understanding when nothing is said—because that says something. Silence is not just empty. Silence has its own messages. Because you are much too filled with thoughts, you cannot understand, you cannot hear that small, still voice within.

Just listen to a cuckoo, the cuckoo's song. Patanjali says listen so meditatively that your thoughts disappear—*nirodh* comes. Not in gaps, showers on you like samadhi. No thoughts interfere, no distraction, one-pointedness arises. Suddenly, you are one with the cuckoo, you understand why she is calling, because we are part of one whole. Behind that sound there is a hidden meaning in the cuckoo's heart: if you are silent, you will be able to understand it.

Patanjali says, 'The sound and the purpose and idea behind it are together in the mind in a confused state. By performing *sanyama* on the sound, separation happens and there arises comprehension of the meaning of sounds made by any living being.'

Mulla Nasruddin stood in an auction room all afternoon waiting for lot 455, which was a South American parrot in a chromium cage. Finally, his chance came and the parrot was put up for sale. The Mulla bought it, but it cost him far more money then he had expected to spend on it. Still, his wife badly wanted one just like it.

As the assistant came down to him to get his name and address, he said, 'You have got yourself a nice bird there, sir.'

The Mulla said, 'I know. He is a beauty. Just one thing, I forgot to ask if that parrot can talk.'

The assistant's eyebrows went up. 'Talk?' he said, 'Hell, he was bidding against you for the last five minutes!'

But we are so occupied in our own thoughts, who listens? Who listens to a parrot? People don't listen to their lovers. Who listens to the wife? Who listens to the husband? Who listens to the father, or who listens to the child? People are so occupied, preoccupied in their heads—hung up—there is no possibility for listening. Listening needs silence. Listening needs attentiveness. Listening needs a deep passivity, a receptivity. It is not absent-mindedness—it is full of attention, full of awareness, full of light: but passive.

ॐ

By observing past impressions, knowledge of previous birth is obtained.

And when you become silent—what Patanjali calls *Ekagrata parinam*, the transformation that brings you one-pointedness of consciousness—when that arises, you can look into your past impressions. You can move backwards and you can go to your past lives. And that is very, very significant, because once you can look into your past lives, you will instantly become different. It is because you have forgotten all that you have lived before, you go on repeating the old nonsense again and again.

If you can see back, you can see again the same pattern, again the same pattern . . . that you were jealous, that you were possessive, that you were full of hate and anger, that you were greedy, that you were trying to become powerful in the world, trying to attain to riches, success, ambition, that you were an egoist again and again and always you failed and always death came and all that you were doing was disrupted, and again you started the same game again . . . If you go back and you can see millions of lives spread all over eternity, can you be the same? Can you still move into greed when you see the frustration that it has been bringing to you?

But we forget. The past is absorbed by ignorance; it moves into a dark night. An oblivion falls, a curtain, and you cannot move back.

The proprietor of an art gallery in Bombay, showing pictures to a customer who did not know what he liked, tried out a landscape, a still life, a portrait, and a floral piece, all without results.

'Would you be interested in a nude?' the proprietor of the gallery asked in desperation. 'Would you be interested in a nude?'

'Good heavens, no,' said the visitor. 'I am a gynaecologist.'

Please don't suspect anything about Dr Phadnis! He has told me not to tell you.

If you are a gynaecologist, how can you be interested in a nude? In fact, it is impossible to be interested in the body. The more you know, the less the fascination. The more you know, the less the obsession. The more you know, the more the futility.

If one can move back into the past impressions of past lives . . . And that is simple: just one-pointedness is needed. Buddha has told his past-life stories, *The Jataka Stories*; they are a treasure. Never before had anybody done that. Each story is significant—because that is the story of all humanity, all humanness, the stupidity of man, the greed, the jealousy, the anger, the compassion, the love. If you can see back, that very vision will change your future. You will not be the same again.

A gentleman in his seventies got his nerve together and took a flight in an airplane. As he climbed out after the ride, he turned to the pilot and said, 'Sir, I wish to thank you for both of those rides.'

'What are you talking about?' said the pilot. 'You had only one ride.'

'No, sir,' said the passenger, 'I had two—my first and my last.'

Experience transforms, but to transform you, the experience needs to be conscious. Unconscious experience cannot change you. You have lived the same pattern that you are living now—many times—but you go on forgetting about it. Then again you start the same rut, as if something new is being started. Many times you have fallen in love, and many times you were frustrated. Again, you are seeking the old ways.

Your body may be new: your mind is not new. Your body is just like a new bottle, and your mind is very old wine. The bottles go on changing and the wine goes on remaining the same.

Patanjali says that if you become one-pointed—and you can become because there is no secret in it; just effort, perseverance, patience is needed—you will be able to see all that you have been before. Just the vision of it, and your pattern will collapse. No miracle in it; it is a simple, natural law.

The problem arises because you are unconscious. The problem arises because you have been dying and being born again and again, but each time, somehow, a curtain falls and your own past is hidden from you. You are like an iceberg, only a small part on the surface and the major part is under the surface. Your personality right now is just a small part protruding out of the surface. All your past is just underneath, underneath the surface. Once you become aware of it, nothing else is needed. That very awareness becomes a revolution.

Quizzing a bunch of recruits, the Marine sergeant asked, 'Jones, when you clean a rifle, what is the first thing you do?'

'Look at the number,' the man replied promptly.

'Now, what on earth has that got to do with cleaning a rifle?' the sergeant demanded.

'Just want to make sure,' replied Jones, 'that I am cleaning my own.'

That is the point which everybody goes on missing. You don't know who you are; you don't know what is your number; you don't know what you have been doing all along. You have become very clever in forgetting things. Now psychoanalysts say that whatsoever is painful, man tends to forget it. Not that you really forget—it remains part of your unconscious. In deep hypnosis it comes up, bubbles up. In deep hypnosis, everything comes back.

For example, if I ask you what you did on the first of January 1961, you cannot remember. You were, of course, there. The first of January 1961, you were alive, all of you were there, but what you did from the morning till the evening you don't remember. Then go to a hypnotist and allow yourself to be hypnotized. In deep hypnosis, he will ask, 'What did you do on the first of January 1961?' And you will relate everything, even the minute details—that you went for a walk in the morning and it was beautiful, and there was dew on the grass, and you can still remember the coldness of the morning, and the hedges were being cut in the garden and you can still remember, you can almost smell again, the fragrance of the new hedges being cut, and the sun rising . . . And small details, minute details, and the whole day as if you again live it. When you are brought out of hypnosis, you have forgotten again.

It seems that to remember all will be too much for you, it will become too much of a burden, so you go on throwing it in the basement of the consciousness. The basement has to be searched because there are hidden treasures also, and the basements have to be searched because only searching through it will you become aware of your foolishness that you have been repeating continuously. You can go beyond it only when you have understood it. A basement understood becomes the passage for a higher story of your being.

Modern psychology says there are two divisions of consciousness: the conscious and the unconscious. Yoga psychology says there is one more division: the superconscious. You live on the ground floor, that is consciousness. Beneath it is a great basement, the unconscious—the whole accumulated past. And when I say the whole accumulated past, I mean all your lives as man, all your lives as animals, all your lives as birds, all your lives as trees, plants, all your lives as rocks, metals—from the very beginning, if there was any beginning, or from the very beginningless beginning. All that has happened to you, all transformations, they are all accumulated in the basement. One has to go through it.

The very understanding will give you the key of the staircase from where you can go to the superconscious.

Patanjali says it happens according to a simple law. All miracles happen according to a simple law; the law when you become one-pointed. There is only one miracle, and that is the miracle of becoming one-pointed.

These sutras are the very base for a future science to develop, one day or another. Now the basic work has started in the West. Much is being done as far as the supersensible is concerned; much is being done for the paranormal. But still everything is in the dark; people are groping. When things become more clear, Patanjali is going to take his right place in the history of human consciousness. He is incomparable—the first scientist who does not believe in any superstition, in any miracle, and who reduces everything to a scientific law.

'*By observing past impressions, knowledge of previous birth is obtained.*' In Primal Therapy, you do a little work on these lines; you go a little backward, up to your birth in this life. That is just spadework. If you succeed in that, you can be helped more deeply; you can be helped to remember the days in the womb. I am going to start a new therapy, Hypnotherapy. Soon, when you have done Primal, and you have succeeded in it, then Hypnotherapy can help you to go deeper, to remember the days in the womb; then go still deeper and to remember your last life, when you died; then go still deeper into your last life's details.

If you can go into one life's detail, you have the key, then you can open all the past doors.

But why open the past doors? Because in the past is hidden the future. If you know your past, you will not repeat it in the future. If you don't know it, you will go on repeating it again and again and again. The very knowledge of the past becomes a guarantee that now you will not repeat it in the future; in the future, you are going to be a totally new man. Yoga is the science of the new man.

ॐ

8. The Rock-Bottom of No and Yes

Osho, once you referred to Sartre, saying that when he was asked in an interview, 'What is the most significant thing in your life?' Sartre replied, 'Everything. To love, to live, to smoke.' And then you remarked that this reply is very Zen-like. But does Sartre have a Zen-consciousness?

THAT'S WHY I said very much Zen-like. Not actually Zen, but very much Zen-like. Existentialism is almost on the verge where it can become Zen. It can go on sticking where it stands now and it will not be a Zen, but it can take the jump and become Zen. Sartre is standing where Buddha was also standing before he became enlightened, but Buddha was open towards the future. He was still searching: he was still on the journey. Sartre has become fixed in his negativity.

The negative is necessary but not enough. That's why I go on saying, unless you are capable of saying no to God, you will never become capable of saying yes. But just to say no is not enough. It is necessary, but one has to move on—from no to yes, from negative to positive.

Sartre is still clinging to the negative, to the no. Good that he has come up to that, but not good enough. One step more, where negativity also disappears, where negativity is also negated. The negation of the negation becomes absolute positive. The negation of the negation is the total yes. Let me explain it to you.

You are sad. You can become settled in your sadness, you can accept it as if 'this is the end', journey stops, no searching, no inquiry anymore—you have settled, you have made your home in the no. Now you are not a process; you have become stagnant. The no has become your lifestyle. Never make anything your lifestyle. If you have attained to no, don't stop there. The search is endless. Go on, go on . . . one day when you have reached to the very rock-bottom of no, you start moving upwards towards the surface. Dive deep into the no. You will reach to the rock-bottom. From there the turning point, then you move in the opposite direction. Then comes the world of yes. Atheist: then you become a theist. Then you say yes to the whole existence. Then sadness turns into a bliss, no becomes yes. But this too is not the end. Go on and on. As no has been left, yes also will disappear.

That is the point of Zen, where yes and no both disappear, and you are left without any attitude. You are left without any idea—naked, nude—just with a clarity, nothing to hinder it—not even a yes. No philosophy, no dogma, no theology, no doctrine—nothing to hinder you, nothing to cloud you. This is what Patanjali calls *nirbeej samadhi*, *seedless samadhi*, because in the yes, the seed can be carried still.

This is the point of transcendence. This is the point where you disappear completely and, at the same time, you become total. This is why Buddha will not say yes to God, will not say no to God. If you ask him, 'Is there God?' he will smile, at the most. That smile shows his transcendence. He will not say yes, he will not say no, because he knows both are stages on the path but not the goal—and both are childish. In fact, anything becomes childish when you cling to it. Only a child clings. A grown-up man leaves all clinging: real maturity is non-clinging—not even to yes.

Buddha is so godlike and so godless. All people who have really attained, go beyond yes and no.

Remember this. Sartre is hanging somewhere at the very border of no. That's why he goes on talking about sadness, depression, anxiety, anguish. All negatives. He has written a great book, his magnum opus, *Being and Nothingness*. In that book he tries to prove that being is nothingness—the total negation. But he clings to it.

But he is an authentic man. His no is true. He has earned it. It is not just a denial of God; he has lived that denial. He has suffered for it; he has sacrificed for it. It is an authentic no.

So there are two types of atheists—as there are always two types in every direction—the authentic and the inauthentic. You can become an atheist for wrong reasons. A communist is an atheist, but he is not authentic. His reasons are false: his reasons are superficial. He has not lived his no.

To live the no is to sacrifice oneself at the altar of negativity, to suffer tremendously, to move in the world of desperation, to move in darkness, to move in the hopeless state of mind where darkness prevails ultimately, endlessly, and there is no hope for any morning—to move into the meaningless and to not, in any way, create any illusion; because the temptation is great. When you are in a dark night, the temptation is great at least to dream about the morning, to think about the morning, to create an illusion around you, to hope for it. And whenever you start hoping, you start trying to believe in it, because you cannot hope without belief. You can hope if you believe. Belief is inauthentic: disbelief is also inauthentic.

Sartre's no is really true. He has lived it; he has suffered for it. He won't cling to any belief. Whatsoever the temptation, he will not dream. Whatsoever the allurement and the fascination of hope and future, of God and heaven, no—he will not be tempted. He will stick. He will remain fixed with the fact. The fact is that there is no meaning. The fact is that there seems to be no God, the sky seems to be empty. The fact is there seems to be no justice. The fact is the whole existence seems to be accidental—not a cosmos but a chaos.

It is difficult to live with this chaos. It is almost impossible—inhuman or superhuman—to live with this chaos and not to start dreaming about it, because one feels as if he is going mad. That's where Nietzsche became mad—the same situation as Sartre is in. He became mad. He was the first of this new mind, the first pioneer man who tried an authentic no. He went mad. Too many people will go mad if they try no—because then there is no love, then there is no hope, then there is no meaning. Your existence is arbitrary, accidental. Inside emptiness, outside emptiness . . . no goal anywhere. Nothing to cling to, nowhere to go—no reason to be.

Seems difficult, almost impossible.

Sartre has earned it; he has lived it. He is a true man—a true Adam. He has disobeyed. He has said no. He has been thrown out of the garden—the garden of hopes, the garden of dreams, the garden of your wish fulfilments. Naked, nude, into the cold world he has lived.

He is a beautiful man, but one step more is needed. A little more courage. He has not yet touched the rock-bottom of nothingness.

Why has he not been able to touch the rock-bottom of nothingness? Because he has made a philosophy out of nothingness. Now that philosophy itself gives him a meaning. He talks about sadness. Have you watched anybody talking about his sadness? His very talk helps the sadness to disappear. That's why people talk about sadness, people talk about their miserable lives. They talk because just the talk, and they forget about it.

He has been talking, arguing, that nothing is meaningful, that the whole life is meaningless. Now this has become his meaning—to argue for it, to fight for it. That is where he has missed the point. A little deeper and the rock-bottom is close by. He will be thrown back towards a deep yes.

Out of no, yes is born. If out of no, yes is not born, something has gone wrong. It has to be so. Out of the night, the morning is born. If the morning is not born, something has gone wrong. Maybe the morning is there but the man has made it a point not to open his eyes. He has become addicted to darkness, or the man has gone blind, or the man has lived in darkness so long that light dazzles him and blinds him.

One step more in this life or in another and Sartre will become a real man of Zen. He will be able to say yes. Out of no, but remember, out of an authentic no.

Have you watched sometimes the phenomenon of false pregnancy? A woman believes that she is pregnant, and just by the belief, just by the idea, she becomes auto-hypnotized that she is pregnant. She starts feeling her belly is growing—and the belly really starts growing. Maybe there is nothing but air. And every month the belly goes on getting bigger and bigger and bigger. Just her mind helping the belly to accumulate air, just the very idea. And there is nothing—no pregnancy, no child inside. This is false pregnancy; there is not going to be any birth.

When somebody says no without earning it, without having lived for it . . . For example, now in Russia, no has become the official philosophy. Everybody is a communist and everybody is an atheist. Now the no is bogus—as bogus as the yes of Indians. It is a false pregnancy now. Now it is the official religion; now it is government propagated. In every school and college and university, now the no is being worshipped. Atheism has become the religion; now everybody is taught about it. The pregnancy is going to be false, conditioned by others; just as in a religious home—Christian, Hindu, Mohammedan—you are born and then you are taught something and, by and by, you start believing.

A small child seeing his father praying starts praying because children are imitative. The father going to the church . . . the child goes to the church. Seeing that everybody believes, he also starts pretending. Now a false pregnancy is born. The belly will go on growing and no child will come out of it, no life will be born out of it. Only, the person will become ugly because of the belly.

The yes can be false, the no can be false; then nothing comes out of it. A tree is known by the fruit, and a cause is known by the effect. Whether you are authentic or not will be known by your rebirth. This is one thing.

The second thing to remember is: you may be really pregnant, but if the mother resists the very idea to give birth to a child, she may kill the child. The child was real, but the mother has to cooperate. When the child wants to come out of the womb after nine months of growth, the mother needs to cooperate.

Because mothers don't cooperate, that's why there is so much pain. Childbirth is such a natural thing, there need not be any pain. In fact, those who know, they say that childbirth will become one of the most ecstatic moments of a woman's life if she cooperates, nothing like it. No sexual orgasm can go so deep as when the woman participates in the process of childbirth. Her whole existence vibrates with a new life; a new being is born. She becomes a vehicle of the divine. She becomes a creator. Every fibre of her being vibrates with a new tune; a new song is heard in the deepest depth of her being. She will be ecstatic.

No sexual orgasm can be so deep as the orgasm that can be attained by a woman when she becomes a mother, but just the opposite is happening. Rather than being ecstatic, a woman passes through tremendous suffering—because she fights. The child is going outward, the child is leaving the womb, he is ready—he is ready to go out into the big world, the wide world—and the mother clings. She is closed, she is not helping, she is not open. If she is *really* closed, she can kill the child.

That is what is happening to Sartre: the child is ready, and he has carried a real pregnancy, but now he is afraid. Now the no itself has become his aim of life, as if pregnancy itself has become the aim, not the child. As if a woman feels so good just carrying a weight in the womb that now she is afraid if the child is born, she will lose something. Pregnancy should not become a style of life. It is a process; it begins and it ends. One should not cling to it. Sartre is clinging; that's where he is missing.

There are many atheists in the world with false pregnancies, very few atheists with real pregnancies. But you can miss even when you have a real pregnancy.

Never make any point of view your philosophy, because once it becomes your philosophy, your ego is involved, and then you go on and on protecting it, arguing for it, searching for proofs to help it.

Amitabh has given a small story. That will be good to understand:

One Jewish sage in Brooklyn asks another Jewish sage, 'What is green, hangs on a wall, and whistles?'

A riddle: what is green, hangs on a wall, and whistles?

The second Jewish sage, contemplating, said, 'I do not know.'

First sage: 'A red herring.'

Second sage, 'But you said it was green.'

First sage, 'You can paint one green. Red herring, but you can paint it.'

Second sage, 'But you said it hangs on the wall.'

First sage, 'Of course, you can hang it on the wall.'

Second sage, 'But you said it whistles!'

First sage, 'So, it does not whistle.'

But one goes on and on. Now nothing is left of the original proposition, but one goes on clinging to it. It becomes an ego trip.

Sartre is an authentic man, but the whole thing has become an ego trip. He needs a little more courage.

Yes. I say to you, to say no needs courage; to say yes needs more courage. Because to say no, ego can be helpful. In every no, ego can be helpful. It feels good to say no; ego feels nourished, strengthened. But to say yes is a surrender; it needs more courage.

Sartre needs a conversion, where the no becomes yes, then he will be not Zen-like; he will be Zen.

And beyond Zen is Buddha. Beyond Zen is Buddha: the ultimate enlightenment, the *nirbeej samadhi* of Patanjali—*seedless samadhi*—where yes is also dropped, because yes is carried against a no. When the no is really dropped, there is no need to carry yes.

Why do you say God is? Because you are still afraid he may not be. Nobody says this is day. Nobody says this is the sun rising, because everybody knows it is so. Whenever you insist, that this is so, somewhere deep in your unconscious there is fear. You are afraid it may not be so. Because of that fear, you go on insisting, saying yes. People become fanatics, dogmatists. They are ready to be killed or to kill for their ideas.

Why is there so much dogmatism in the world? Because people have not attained, really. They are afraid. They are afraid—anybody who says no, creates a temptation for them. They also carry their no within, still. If somebody says no, their no starts being alive, and they are afraid of themselves. They live a closed life so that nobody disturbs their ideology.

But a man who has really attained to yes, what is the need to say yes? Buddha does not say anything about God. He simply smiles at the whole stupidity of yes and no. Life is there without any interpretation. It is complete—*utterly* complete and perfect. No ideology is needed to say anything about it. You have to be silent and still to listen to it. You have to be in it to feel it and live it. Always remember, people who are obsessed too much with yes must be suppressing some no within their being.

ॐ

It is from Amitabh:

> Herman Hesse's *Siddhartha* speaks thus to Buddha: 'O illustrious one, in one thing above all have I admired your teachings. Everything is completely clear and proved. You show the world as a complete, unbroken chain—an eternal chain. Completely coherent, embracing the big and the small from the same stream. Not for one moment do I doubt that you are Buddha, that you have reached the highest which so many thousand are striving to reach. You have done so by your own seeking, in your own way. You have learned nothing through teachings, and so I think, O illustrious one, that no one finds salvation through teachings, to nobody can you communicate in your teachings what happened to you in the moment of your enlightenment. The secret of what the Buddha himself experienced—he alone among hundreds of thousands. This is why I am going on my way—not to seek another and better teacher, for there are none better, but to reach alone— or die.' Would you comment?

Herman Hesse's *Siddhartha* is one of the very rare books, something from his innermost depth. Never again could

Hesse bring another jewel more beautiful and more precious than *Siddhartha*; as if he was spent in it. He could not reach higher. *Siddhartha* is Hesse's height.

Siddhartha is saying to Buddha, 'Whatsoever you say is true. How can it be otherwise? You have explained everything that was never explained before; you have made everything clear. You are the greatest teacher there is. But you attained to this enlightenment on your own. You were not a disciple. You were not following anybody; you searched alone. You came to this enlightenment alone, walking a path, not following anybody.' 'I must leave you,' says Siddhartha to Gautam Buddha, 'not to find a greater teacher than you, because there is none, but to seek the truth on my own. Only with this teaching I agree'— because this is Buddha's teaching, 'Be a light unto yourself.' Follow nobody; seek and search, but follow nobody. 'With this I agree,' says Siddhartha, 'so I will have to go.'

He is sad. It must have been very difficult for him to leave Buddha, but he has to go—to seek, to search, or to die. He has to find the path.

What is my comment on it? There are two types of people in the world. 99 per cent who cannot go alone . . . Alone, if they try, they will remain fast asleep for ever and ever. Alone, left to themselves, the possibility is nil. They will need somebody to wake them; they will need somebody to shake them out of their sleep, to shock them. They will need somebody to help them. But there is another type also, that is only 1 per cent, which can find its way on its own.

Buddha belongs to the first type: the rare type, the 1 per cent. Siddhartha also belongs to the same type. He understands Buddha, he loves Buddha, he reveres him. He feels the sadness and the pain and the heartache when leaving him, but he knows he has to leave. He has to find his own way. He has to seek the truth on his own. He cannot become a shadow; that is not possible for him, that is not his type. But that does not mean that everybody has to seek on his own.

In this century there have been two very important persons: Gurdjieff and Krishnamurti. They are the types. Krishnamurti goes on insisting everybody has to be on his own. Alone one has to seek and alone one has to reach. And Gurdjieff insisted that schoolwork is needed—alone you will never be able to escape out of the prison. All the prisoners have to come together to fight with the forces which are guarding, which have made the prison. And all the prisoners have to get together to find ways and means and methods—and they need somebody's support who is outside the prison. Otherwise, they will not find the way; they will not find how to get out. Somebody who was in the prison and has somehow reached out, his help is needed, that is the master.

Who is right? Krishnamurti's followers won't listen to Gurdjieff, Gurdjieff's followers won't listen to Krishnamurti, and the followers go on thinking that the other is wrong. But I tell you, both are right because humanity has two types.

And none is better. Don't try to evaluate. Somebody is a woman and somebody is a man—nobody is higher and nobody is lower; different types of biology. Somebody is who can find alone and somebody is who needs help—nobody is higher and nobody is lower; different types of spirituality.

The person who cannot find alone is the person for

whom surrender will be the path, love will be the path, devotion will be the path, trust will be the path. Don't think that trust is easy. It is as difficult as to follow on your own, sometimes even more difficult. And there are people who will follow alone.

Just a few days before, a young man came and he asked me, 'Can I not search on my own? Need I be a sanyasi? Need I be a disciple to you? Can I not follow on my own, can I not search on my own?' I said, 'Why have you come to ask me? You are not the type who follows on his own. Even *this* you cannot decide. What more will you be able to decide on your own? This too you have come to ask me. This I have to decide—already you are a disciple!' But he argued; he said, 'But you never were a disciple to any master.' I said, 'That's right, but I never went to ask any. Even for this, I never went to ask any.'

And this is my understanding: that people who have followed on their own rarely achieve, very rarely—because many times your ego will say that you are the rare type, that you can go on your own, alone, no need to follow anybody: and your ego will deceive you. You may not follow anybody; you are following your own ego, your own image, and it is going to lead you into a thousand and one ditches. You are following yourself, in fact. You are not moving on your own; you are following yourself. And you are a confused chaos. Where will you go? How will you go?

Be very clear about it. Listen to your innermost depths. Is it the ego which says don't be a follower? If it is the ego, you are not going to be going anywhere. You are trapped, already trapped. Then it is good to follow somebody. Find a school, find a master. Drop this ego because this ego will lead you into more and more nonsense and rubbish.

Look at Siddhartha's words. He says, 'This is why I am going on my way—not to seek another and better teacher, for there are none better . . .' He loves Buddha tremendously; he respects him tremendously. He says, 'Whatsoever you say is absolutely clear. Nobody has taught in such a clear way ever before. Whatsoever you say about the small and the big, it is absolutely comprehensible, appeals, converts, creates a sympathy for it. I *know*,' he says, 'you have attained. I am not going away from you because I suspect you, no. I respect you. I have seen the glimpse through you; I have looked through you into reality. I am grateful, but I have to go.'

His type is not of that who can become a follower. He goes into the world, he moves into the world. He lives with a prostitute. He tries to know what indulgence is. He learns the ways of the world and the ways of sin and, by and by, out of many sufferings, many disappointments, frustrations, the consciousness arises in him. Long is his path, but he goes on unflinching, unwavering. Whatsoever the cost, he is ready either to die or to attain. He has understood his type.

To understand one's type is the most basic thing in spiritual search. If you are confused about what type you are—because people come to me; they say, 'You say to understand the type is the most important thing, but we don't know what type we are'—remain certain: you are not that type who can go on his own. Because you cannot be certain even about your type, that too has to be decided by somebody else, then you will not be able to go alone. Then drop that ego. That is simply ego.

It has happened . . . Pitfalls are many. If you go and

watch Krishnamurti's disciples, you will see almost all the wrong type gather together. Not people like Siddhartha—because why should they go to Krishnamurti? Wrong people—who need a teacher—and still are not ready to drop their egos; you will find them around Krishnamurti. It is a beautiful arrangement. Krishnamurti says, 'I am not a teacher'; so their egos are intact. He does not say, 'Surrender'; so there is no trouble. In fact, he enhances their egos: that 'you are to find your path alone.' They feel beautiful, and they go on listening to Krishnamurti for years and years and years.

There are people who have been listening to him for forty years. Sometimes they come to me and I ask them, 'If really you have understood him, why don't you stop going to him?—because he says there is no teacher and he is not your teacher and there is nothing to be taught and nothing to be learned; one has to search through life through the hard way; one has to reach oneself. Why have you wasted forty years?' And I can see in their faces the problem is they need a master but they don't want to surrender. So this is a good compromise: Krishnamurti says no need to surrender, and he goes on teaching, and they go on listening and learning.

With Gurdjieff you will find a better group than with Krishnamurti—people who can surrender, who are ready to surrender. There are loopholes also because there are people who don't want to do anything, and when they don't want to do anything, they think this is surrender. There are people who are suckers, who don't want to do anything. They say, 'We surrender. Now this is your responsibility. Now if something goes wrong, you are responsible.' But Gurdjieff won't allow such people. He was very hard. He will create so many difficulties for them that they will escape within hours. Only very rare people will be there who have really surrendered.

For example, one man came, a musician, a very accomplished musician who was already known, famous for his art: and Gurdjieff says, 'Stop music and start digging holes in the garden.' And twelve hours per day. That man has never done such hard work. He has always played on the organ. His hands are delicate; they are not those of a labourer: they are not of a manual worker. Delicate, feminine hands, they know only one work—they can touch the keys of the organ. That's all he has done his whole life, and now this man says . . . But he started digging the next morning.

By the evening comes Gurdjieff and he says, 'Good, very good. Now throw the earth back into the holes. Fill the holes. And unless you have filled them, don't go to sleep.' So again four, five hours he has to fill all the holes— as they were—because in the morning he will come to see. In the morning, he is there and he says, 'Good. Now dig other holes.' And this goes on for three months.

Absurd activity, but if you have surrendered, you have surrendered. You don't need to bother about what he is doing. You have to surrender reasoning.

After three months that man has grown into a totally different being. Then Gurdjieff said, 'Now you can play music.' A new music has arisen; it was never there before. He has touched something of the unknown. He followed, he trusted, he went with Gurdjieff the whole way.

People who are trying to deceive will not stay there; they will immediately escape. With Krishnamurti, they can stay, because nothing to work, nothing to meditate . . .

And Krishnamurti is right! But he is right only for 1 per cent, and this is the problem that 1 per cent will never go to listen to him. That 1 per cent moves on his own. If he somehow comes across Krishnamurti, he will thank him. This is what Siddhartha did.

Siddhartha had come across Buddha. He listened to him, he felt the beauty, he felt the tremendous significance of whatsoever he was saying, he felt this man, he felt his attainment, he felt his enlightenment, his meditative energy also touched his heart, near him he felt the call of the unknown: but he understands his type. With deep respect, with deep love, in sadness, he departs. He says, 'I would have liked being with you, but I know I have to go.' He goes not because of the ego. He goes not to seek another greater teacher. He goes because he knows that he cannot be a follower. There is no resistance in him; he listened without resistance; he understood Buddha. He understood so totally, that's why he had to go.

If Krishnamurti is understood *really* then you have to go. Then he is not the man to be around; then you have to go. You can be with Gurdjieff. You cannot be with Krishnamurti, because his whole teaching is to go alone, follow no path—truth is pathless, the gate is gateless—the method is only one and that is to be aware. Nothing else is to be done. Once you have understood, you will feel thankful, you will pay your respects, and you will move on your way. But this is only for 1 per cent of the people.

And, remember, if you are not of that type, don't pretend to be, because you cannot change your type. That is impossible. You have to use your type, and through using your type, you have to go beyond.

♂

*If there is no personal God, why do you answer
my thoughts every morning? If the listening is
there, will the process continue when I return to
the West?*

Yes, I answer your thoughts every morning whether you
ask me or not, whether you write questions or not. I
answer your thoughts because there is no personal God.
What do I mean?

If there is a personal god, he will be much too occupied;
it will be impossible to answer your questions. He will be
much too occupied—the problems of the whole universe.
This earth is not alone. Just think. If a person, a personal
god, has to think about the problems and the anxieties and
the worries and the questions only about this earth, then
too he will go mad—and this earth is nothing. This earth
is just a speck of dust. Scientists say that it is almost certain
that there must be 50,000 earths with as much evolved life
as this earth in the universe, and that is an understatement—
50,000 earths as much evolved as this earth, even more
evolved. The more we can penetrate into the universe, the
more boundaries go away—and far away. The boundaries
have disappeared; it is an unbounded universe. If there is
a personal god, either he would have gone mad long
before, or he would have committed suicide.

Because there is not a personal god, things are simple.
The whole existence is divine. There is no anxiety; nothing
is overcrowded. Divineness is spread all over existence, not
confined in a personal god.

When I answer your questions, if I am a person, it will
be difficult. Then you are many and I am one. If all your
minds jump on my mind, I will go mad. But because there
is nobody inside, madness is not possible. I am just an

empty valley, echoing. Not that there is somebody who echoes, just the empty valley echoing. Or I am just a mirror. You come in front of me, you are mirrored. You are gone, the reflection is gone.

I am not here in any personal way, just an emptiness; so it is not an effort on my part to answer your questions or your thoughts. Simply, because you are there, I reflect you. And this is not an effort.

Somebody asked Michelangelo, 'In your work there seems to be great inspiration.' He said, 'Yes, there is—but only 1 per cent. 1 per cent inspiration and 99 per cent perspiration.' And he is right. With me, there is no perspiration. It is a 100 per cent inspiration. I am not thinking about your problems. I am not thinking about you at all. I am not worried about you. I am not trying to help you. You are there. I am here: just between the two, something transpires—between my nothingness and your beingness, something transpires which has nothing to do with me and which has nothing to do with you. Just an empty valley, and you sing a song, and the valley repeats, and the valley resounds it.

So it will make no difference whether you are here or in the West. If you feel any difference, that will be because of you, not because of me. When you are close to me, you feel more open. Just your idea, that because you are here, you feel more open. Then you go to the West, just your idea that now you are too far away, how can you be open—you become closed. Just drop that idea, and wherever you are, I am available; because this availability is not personal, so it is not a question of time and space. Go to the West, go to the farthest end of the earth, but remain in the same attitude.

Just try. Many of you will be going. Every morning, eight o'clock Indian time, just come as you come here, sit as you sit here, wait as you wait here, and immediately, you will start feeling your thoughts are being answered. And it will be an even more beautiful experience than being close to me because then there will be nothing physical. It will be totally transcendental; it will be the purest possible. And then if you can do that, space disappears. Between a master and a disciple, there is no space.

And then another miracle is possible: then one day you can drop time also. Because some day, I will leave this body; I will not be here. If you have not transcended time before I leave my body, I will become unavailable to you. Not that I will be unavailable. I will remain available, but just your idea that now I am dead, so how can you relate to me . . . you will become closed.

It is your idea. Drop that idea of time and space. So first try eight o'clock in the morning, Indian standard time, wherever you are, and then drop that Indian standard time also. Then try any time. First drop space, then drop time. And you will be so ecstatic to find that I am available wherever you are. Then there is no question.

Buddha died. Many started crying and weeping, but there were a few who just sat there. Manjushree was there, one of his great disciples. He was sitting under the tree; he remained the same. He heard, as if nothing has happened. It was one of the greatest events in the history of the world. Rarely a buddha is born, so there is no question of buddha dying; rarely it happens. Somebody came to Manjushree and he said, 'What are you doing? Are you shocked so much that you cannot move? Buddha is dead!' Manjushree laughed and he said, 'Before he died, I dropped time and space. He will remain available to me wherever he is, so don't bring such absurd news to me.' He never followed, he never went to see the dead body. He is quite at ease, relaxed. He knows that that availability was not confined to time or to space.

Buddha has remained available to those who are available to him. I will remain available to you if you are available to me, so learn how to be available to me.

℘

> *Osho, your answer about the heart which was approximately yogi reminded me of the following interchange:*
>
> *Wife: 'Darling, Since we married, do you love me more, or less?'*
>
> *Husband: 'More or less.'*

To ask about love in terms of more or less is stupid, because love can neither be more nor less. Either it is or it is not. It is not a quantity; it is a quality. It cannot be measured; it is immeasurable. You cannot say more, you cannot say less. The question is irrelevant, but lovers go on asking because they don't know what love is. Whatsoever they know must be something else. It cannot be love because love is not quantitative. How can you love *more*? How can you love *less*?

Either you love or you don't love.

Love surrounds you, fills you totally, or disappears completely and is not there . . . not even a trace is left behind. Love is a totality. You cannot divide it; division is not possible. Love is indivisible. If you have not come across such love which is indivisible, be alert. Then whatsoever you have been thinking is love is a counterfeit coin. Drop it—sooner the better—and search for the real coin.

And what is the difference? The difference is when you love as a counterfeit coin, you are simply imagining that you love. It is a trick of the mind. You imagine that you love—just as in the night, you have been hungry the whole day, fasting, and you go to sleep, and you dream that you are eating. Because man lives in such a loveless life, the mind goes on dreaming about love and creating false, absolutely false, dreams around you. They help you to live somehow, and that's why again and again dreams are broken, love is shattered, and again you start creating another dream—but never becoming aware that these dreams are not going to help.

Somebody asked Gurdjieff how to love. He said, 'First *be*. Otherwise all love will be false.' If you are authentically there, really there, in full awareness, in concrete beingness, only then is love possible.

Love is like a shadow to a real being. Only a Buddha, a Christ, a Patanjali can love. You cannot love. Love is a function of being. You are still not a being; you are not aware enough to be in love.

Love needs the greatest awareness. Unconscious, asleep, snoring, you cannot love. Your love is more like hate than like love, that's why your love can go sour in a single minute. Your love becomes jealousy any moment. Your love can become hatred any moment. Your love is not love enough. Your love is more like a hiding place, not an open sky. It is more a need, not like an independent flow. More like dependence—and all dependencies are ugly. Real love makes you free, gives you total freedom. It is unconditional. It asks for nothing. It simply gives and shares, and it is happy because the sharing was possible. It is thankful because you accepted.

It asks nothing. Much comes to it, that is another thing, but it asks nothing.

How is it possible to you right now? You are not there to flow. So you go on deceiving. Not only that you deceive others, you deceive basically yourself. And that's why it is always happening. This anecdote is almost an everyday thing in every marriage. The husband is always worried whether the wife loves him or not. The wife is worried whether the husband loves her or not—more or less; how much he loves.

Never ask this question. Always ask, do you love? because it is not a question of the other. How much he loves. How much she loves, is a wrong question. Always ask, do you love? And if you don't love, seek to become more authentic, become more a being, true.

And sacrifice everything for it! It is worth it. All that you have is useless unless you have love. Sacrifice everything for it. Nothing is more valuable. All your Kohinoors are worthless unless you have attained to that quality which is called love. Then God is not needed: love is enough.

Sometimes I see that if people really love, the word 'god' will disappear from the world: there will be no need. Love will be such a fulfilment it will replace God. Now people go on talking about God because they are so unfulfilled in their lives. Love has not been there and they are trying with God, but God is a dead thing—a marble statue, cold, not alive at all.

Love is the real God. Love is the only God. And you cannot have God more or less—either you have or you have not. But search, a deep search is needed: a constant alertness is needed.

And remember one thing, if you can love, you will be fulfilled. If you can love, you will be able to celebrate, you will be able to feel grateful, you will be able to thank with your full heart. If you are capable of love, just being alive is a tremendous delight. Nothing more is needed: it is benediction.

ॐ

9. Into the Fantastic

Through sanyama the image occupying another's mind can be known. But perception through sanyama does not bring knowledge of the mental factors that support the image in another mind for that is not the object of sanyama. By performing sanyama on the form of the body to suspend receptive power, the contact between the eye of an observer and the light from the body is broken, and the body becomes invisible. This principle also explains the disappearance of sound.

'I AM BEGINNING to lose faith in my ability,' said the young salesman to his friend. 'Today has been terrible, and not one sale. I have been thrown out of apartments, had doors slammed in my face, been kicked down staircases, had my samples thrown in the gutter, and been shot at by irate householders.'

His friend asked, 'What is your line?'

'Bibles,' said the young salesman.

Why has religion become a dirty word? Why are people

full of hatred the moment you mention the word religion, God, or something like that? Why has the whole of humanity become indifferent? Something must have gone wrong somewhere. It has to be understood because this is not an ordinary matter.

Religion is such a significant phenomenon that man cannot live without it. And to live without religion will be living without any purpose. To live without religion will be living without any poetry. To live without religion will be living a drag of a life, a boredom—what Sartre is saying when he says that man is a useless passion. Without religion, he becomes so. Man is not a useless passion, but without religion, he certainly becomes so. If there is nothing higher than you, all purpose disappears. If there is nothing higher to reach, higher to be, your life cannot have any goal, cannot have any meaning. The higher is needed to attract you, to pull you upwards. The higher is needed so that you don't get stuck in the lower.

Without religion, life will be like a tree which never comes to flower, a fruitlessness. Yes, without religion, man is a useless passion, but with religion, man becomes the very flowering of life, as if God is fulfilled in him. So it has to be understood why religion has become such a dirty word.

There are people who are positively against religion. There are people who may not be positively against but who are positively indifferent towards religion. There are people who may not be indifferent to religion but who are only hypocrites who go on pretending that they are interested. And these three categories are all the categories there are. A genuine religious person has disappeared. What has happened?

First thing, the discovery of a new attitude towards life, the discovery of science—a new window opened—and religion could not absorb it. Religion failed to absorb because ordinary religion is incapable of absorbing it.

There are three attitudes possible towards life: one is logical, rational, scientific; another is infralogical, superstitious, irrational; and the third is suprarational, transcendental. The ordinary religion tried to cling to the infrarational attitude. That became the suicide; that became the slow poisoning. Religion has committed suicide because it got stuck in the lowest standpoint towards life— infrarational. What do I mean when I use the word 'infrarational'? Just a blind faith. Religion thrived on it up to this century because there was no competitor, there was not a higher standpoint.

When science came into being, a higher standpoint, more mature, more valid, came into existence, there was a conflict. Religion became apprehensive, afraid, because the new attitude was going to destroy it. It became defensive. It became more and more closed. It tried in the beginning— because it was powerful, it was the establishment—it tried to destroy the Galilee's of science, not knowing that those destructive steps were going to become suicidal to itself. Religion started a long battle with science—of course, a losing battle.

No lower standpoint can fight with a higher standpoint. The lower standpoint is bound to fail—today, or tomorrow, or the day after tomorrow. The battle at the most can postpone the defeat, but it cannot avoid it. Whenever a higher standpoint is there, the lower has to disappear. It has to change; it has to become more mature.

Religion died because it could not become more mature.

Ordinary religion, the so-called religion, has died because it cannot raise itself to Patanjali's level. Patanjali is religious and scientific. Only the religion of Patanjali can survive. Less than that won't do now. Man has tasted a higher consciousness through science, more validity about truth. Now man cannot be forced to remain blind and superstitious; it is impossible. Man has come of age. He cannot be forced to be a child in the old ways, and that's what religion has been doing.

It has become a dirty word, naturally.

The second attitude, the logical attitude, is Patanjali's standpoint. He does not ask to believe in anything. He says, be experimental. He says that all that is said is hypothetical—you have to prove it through your experience and there is no other proof. Don't believe in others and don't remain with borrowed knowledge.

Religion died because it became just a borrowed knowledge. Jesus says, 'God is,' and Christians go on believing. Krishna says, 'God is,' and Hindus go on believing. And Mohammed says, 'God is, and I have encountered him and I have heard his voice,' and Mohammedans go on believing. This is borrowed. Patanjali differs there. He says, 'Nobody's experience can be yours. You will have to experience. Only then—and only then—is truth revealed to you.'

I was reading an anecdote:

Two American soldiers were squatting in a dugout somewhere in the Far East waiting for the attack. One of them drew out paper and pencil and started to write a letter, but he broke the point of the pencil. Turning to the other soldier, he said, 'Hey, Mac, can you lend me your ball pen?' The man handed him a ball pen. 'Hey, Mac,' said the letter writer, 'do you happen to have an envelope?' The other man found a crumpled envelope in his pocket and handed it over. The writer scribbled on, then he looked up and said, 'Got a stamp?' He was given a stamp. He folded the letter, put it into the envelope, stuck the stamp on top, then he said, 'Hey, Mac, what is your girl's address?'

Everything borrowed—even the girl's address.

The address that you have got of God is borrowed. That God may have been a girlfriend to Jesus, but he is not to you. That God may have been a beloved to Krishna, but he is not to you. Everything borrowed—the Bible, the Koran, the Gita. How can one go on deceiving oneself by borrowed experience? One day or another the whole thing will look absurd, meaningless. One day or another the borrowed is going to become a burden. It will cripple you and crush you. This has happened.

Patanjali does not believe in borrowed experience. He does not believe in belief. That's his scientific attitude. He believes in experience; he believes in experiment. Patanjali can be understood by Galileo, by Einstein. Galileo and Einstein can be understood by Patanjali. They are fellow-travellers.

The future belongs to Patanjali. It does not belong to the Bible, it does not belong to the Koran, it does not belong to the Gita: it belongs to the *Yoga Sutras*—because he talks in the same language. Not only that he talks, he belongs to the same dimension, the same understanding of life and the same logical approach.

There is a third standpoint also: that is suprarational.

That is the standpoint of Zen. Far away. Very far away in the future. That far away looks like just imagination. There may come a time when Zen may become the world religion, but it is very, very far away, because Zen is suprarational. Let me explain it to you.

The infrarational, that which is below reason, also has an appearance of the suprarational. It looks like it, but it is not like it: it is a counterfeit coin. Both are illogical, but in a tremendously different way. Profound is the difference, vast is the difference. The infrarational is one who lives below reason in the darkness of a blind faith, lives on borrowed knowledge, has not been daring enough to experiment, has not been courageous enough to move into the unknown on his own. His whole life is a borrowed life, inauthentic—dull, drab, insensitive. The man who has moved to the suprarational is also illogical, irrational, but in a totally different sense; his irrationality has absorbed reason and gone higher than it. He has transcended reason.

The man of infrarationality will always be afraid of reason because reason will always create a defensiveness. It will always create a fear. There is the danger if reason succeeds then the faith, then the belief, will have to die— one clings to it *against* reason. The man of suprareason is not afraid of rationality. He can delight in it. The higher plane can always accept the lower—not only accept: it can absorb it: it can nourish on it. It can stand on its shoulders. It can use it. The lower is always afraid of the higher.

The infrarational is a minus thing—minus reason. The suprarational is a plus thing—plus reason. The infrarational is faith. The suprarational is trust—trust through experience. It is not borrowed: but the man of the suprarational has come to understand that life is more than reason. The reason is accepted: there is no denial of it. The reason is good as far as it goes, it has to be used, but life is not finished there. This is not the boundary of life: life is a bigger thing. Reason is part of it—beautiful if it remains in the organic unity of the whole: ugly if it becomes a separate phenomenon and starts functioning on its own. If it becomes an island, then ugly. If it remains part of the vast continent of being, then beautiful: it has its uses.

The man of suprareason is not against the rational: he is beyond the rational. He sees that the rational and the irrational both are part of life like day and night, like life and death. To him, opposites have disappeared and they have become complementaries.

Zen is a transcendental attitude. Patanjali is a very logical attitude. If you move with Patanjali, by and by, in the ultimate peaks you will reach to the suprarational. In fact, just as ordinary religious people are afraid of science and reason and logic; people who cling to the scientific attitude, they are afraid of Zen. You can read Arthur Koestler's books, a very logical man, but he seems to be in the same plight as are ordinary religious people. Now logic has become religion to him: he is afraid of Zen. Whatsoever he writes about Zen has a trembling in it, a fear, an apprehension—because Zen destroys all categories.

Ordinary Christianity, Hinduism, Mohammedanism, they are below reason. Extraordinary Christians—Eckhart, Bohme—Sufis, Kabir, they are beyond reason.

Patanjali can be a bridge for an ordinary human being, ordinarily religious, to move towards Zen. He is the bridge; there exists no other bridge. Patanjali is the scientist of the inner. Man can live two types of lives: a life which is exterior, a life of exteriority: and man can live another type of life: a life which is interior, a life of interiority. Patanjali is the bridge. What he calls *sanyama* is a balance between the exterior and the interior; to come to such a balance that you just stand in between; you can move out, you can come in; nothing is blocking your way; you are available to both the worlds.

In that sense, Patanjali is a greater scientist than Einstein. Someday or the other, Einstein will have to learn from Patanjali. Patanjali has nothing to learn from Einstein because whatsoever you know of the outside world remains, at the most, information. It can never become real knowledge, because you remain outside of it. Real knowledge is possible only when you have to come to the very source of knowing—and there happens the greatest miracle, and many miracles.

The greatest miracle is that the moment you come to the very source of knowing, you disappear. The closer you come to the source, the more you start to disappear. Once centred, you are no more; and yet, for the first time, you are. You are no more as you used to think about yourself. You are no more the ego, that trip is over. For the first time, you are a being.

And with this being, the greatest miracle has happened to you: you have come home. That's what Patanjali calls *samadhi*. *Samadhi* means all problems solved, all questions dissolved, all anxieties resolved. One has come home. In total rest, in total tranquility, nothing disturbs, nothing distracts. Now you are available to enjoy. Now every moment becomes a sheer delight.

First thing, religion got hooked in the infrarational. Second thing, so-called religious people became more and more inauthentic—all their belief became borrowed. And third thing, the world became much too impatient. People are in such a hurry—going nowhere, but in a great hurry. Moving faster and faster and faster and faster. Don't ask them, 'Where are you going?' because that becomes an embarrassing thing. Don't ask them. Just ask, 'How fast are you going?' To ask, 'Where are you going?' is uncivil, unmannerly, because nobody knows where he is going.

People are in a hurry, and religion is such a tree that it needs patience. It needs infinite patience. It needs no-hurry. If you are in a hurry, you will miss what religion is. Why has this so great hurry been created in the modern life? From where has it come? Because in such a hurry, you can, at the most, play with things; you can at the most play with objects. Subjectivity needs long patience, a waiting. It grows, but not in a hurry. It is not a seasonal flower. You cannot get it, and within a month, it is flowering. It takes time. It is the eternal tree of life. You cannot do it in a hurry.

That's why, more and more people become interested in things, because you can get them immediately, and people become less and less interested in persons. With their own person they are not related, and with others' person also they are not related. In fact, people use persons like things and people love things like persons.

I know a man who says he loves his car. He cannot be so certain about his wife—he is not. He cannot so certainly say, 'I love my wife,' but he loves his car. He uses his wife and loves his car. The whole thing has gone upside down.

Use things: love persons. But to love another person, first you will have to become a person. That takes time: that takes long preparation.

That's why people become afraid when they read Patanjali; it seems to be a long process. It is.

I was reading . . .

It happened that one insomniac was delighted when his doctor gave him such an inexpensive prescription for getting to sleep.

'One apple before bedtime,' said the doc.

'Wonderful!' the patient started to leave.

'Wait, that's not all,' cautioned the doctor. 'It must be eaten in a certain way.' The insomniac paused to listen to the rest of the prescription. 'Cut the apple in half,' said the doctor. 'Eat one half, then put on your coat and hat and go out and walk three miles. When you return home, eat the other half.'

No short cuts exist. Don't be befooled by short cuts: life knows no short cuts. It is a long way, and the long way has a certain meaning, because only in that long awaiting do you grow, and you grow gracefully.

The modern mind is in too much of a hurry. Why? What is the hurry? Because the modern mind is much too ego-centred. From there comes the hurry. The ego is always afraid of death—and the fear is natural because the ego is going to die. Nobody can save it. You can protect it for the time being, but nobody can save it forever. It is going to die. You as separate will have to die, and the more you feel that you are separate from existence, from the totality, the more you become afraid. The fear comes because of the separation. The more you become individualistic, the more anxiety-ridden.

In the East, where people are not so individualistic,

where people are still in a primitive state, where people are still part of the collective, where individuality is not insisted upon so much; they are not in a hurry. They move slowly, they take time: they enjoy the journey. In the West, where ego is insisted upon too much and everybody starts to be an individual, more and more anxiety, more and more mental disease, more and more trembling and fear and anguish, more and more apprehension about death. The more you are individualistic, the more you are going to die. The death is always in proportion to your individuality because only the individual dies.

The universal in you goes on living. It cannot die. It was there before you were born; it will be there when you are gone.

I have heard a very beautiful anecdote:

'Yes,' said the boastful man, 'my family can trace its ancestry back to the Mayflower.'

'I suppose,' remarked his friend, sarcastically, 'next you will be telling us that your ancestors were in the ark with Noah.'

'Certainly not,' said the other. 'My people had a boat of their own.'

The ego goes on and on and on, separating you. This separation is the cause of death.

Then you are in a hurry because death is coming—life is short, time is short, many things to do. Who has time to meditate? Who has time to move into the world of yoga? People think these things are only for crazy people. Who is interested in Zen? Because if you meditate, you will have to wait years and years in a very intense, passionate, but passive awareness. You will have to go on waiting. To a Western mind—or to a modern mind because modern mind is Western—to a modern mind, this seems a sheer wastage of time. That's why the flower of religion has become impossible.

People go on pretending that they are religious, but they avoid real religion. It has become a social formality. People go to the church, to the temple, just to be respectable. Nobody takes religion sincerely—because who has time? Life is short and many things to do. People are more interested in things: having a bigger car, having a bigger house, having more money in the bank balance. People have completely forgotten that the real business is to have more being. The real business of life is to have more being—not more bank balance, because the bank balance will remain here. You will be gone. Only your being can go with you.

Yoga is the science of your innermost being, the science of subjectivity, the science of how to grow more . . . how to be more . . . how really to become a god so that you are one with the whole.

ॐ

Now the sutras.

> *Through sanyama the image occupying another's mind can be known.*

If you attain to one-pointedness, if you attain to *samadhi*, and if you become so deeply silent that not a single thought moves in your mind, you become capable of seeing the images in other people's minds. You can read their thoughts.

I have heard a joke that two yogis met. Both have

attained to *samadhi*. There was nothing to talk about, but one has to say something when you meet. One yogi said, 'I would like to share a joke with you. It is very old. Once—' And the other started laughing.

That's the whole joke. He could see the whole joke unuttered.

If you are silent, through your silence, you become capable of seeing into another's mind. Not that you have to, not that you should do it. Patanjali is saying everything that comes on the way. In fact, a real yogi never does it because that is trespassing the freedom of the other, that is violating the privacy of the other; but it happens.

And Patanjali in this chapter 'Vibhuti Pada' is talking about all these miracles; not that one should strive to attain them, but just to make you aware and alert that they happen and don't get caught by them, and don't use them—because once you start using them, your growth stops. The energy then is stuck there. Don't use them. These sutras are to make you alert and aware that these things will happen, and there is a tendency in the mind, a temptation to use them. Who would not like to see into another's mind? You have tremendous power then over the other, but yoga is not a power trip, and a real yogi will never do it.

But it happens. There are people who try to attain it, and it can be attained. It can be attained even without being religious. Even without being a real disciple of yoga, it can be attained.

Sometimes it happens just by accident also. If your mind comes to a silent stage in any way, you are capable of looking into the images of the other's mind, because when your mind is silent, the other's mind is not very far away. It is very close. When your mind is crowded with thoughts, the other's mind is very far away because the crowd of your own thoughts distracts you. The noise of your own inner traffic is so much, you cannot hear the other's thought.

Have you watched it? Sometimes ordinary people, not concerned with meditation, not concerned with yoga or any telepathic powers or any supraphysical sensibilities, sometimes become aware of certain things happening to them. For example, if a couple loves each other deeply, by and by, they become so attuned to each other, they start becoming aware of the other's thoughts. The wife becomes aware of what is moving in the mind of the husband. She may not be aware of this awareness, but in a subtle way she starts feeling what is happening to the mind of the husband. She may not be clear, it may be a confused picture, may not be in focus, may be a little blurred, but lovers, by and by, become aware of a certain capacity to feel the other. The mother, if she loves the child, becomes aware of the needs of the child—unuttered.

There is a path somewhere by which you are connected with the other. We are connected with the whole.

Patanjali says, 'Through *sanyama*,' attaining to one-pointedness, to the inner balance, to *samadhi*, to silence and tranquility, 'the image occupying another's mind can be known.' You have just to focus yourself towards the other. Just in deep silence you have to remember the other. Just in deep silence you have to look at the other and, immediately, you will see his mind opening before you like a book.

But no need to do it. Because once this becomes possible, many more possibilities surround it. You can interfere, you can direct the other's thoughts. You can enter into the other's thoughts and put your thoughts there. You can manipulate the other and he will never become aware that he has been manipulated and he will think he is doing his own thoughts and he is following his own ideas. But these things are not to be done.

ॐ

But perception through sanyama does not bring knowledge of the mental factors that support the image in another's mind, for that is not the object of sanyama.

You can see the image—that doesn't mean that you will see the motive also. For motive you will have to go still deeper. For example, you see somebody and you can see the image inside the mind; for instance, there is an image of the moon, beautiful full moon, surrounded by white clouds. You can see the image, this is okay, but you don't know the motivation why the image is there. If he is a painter, the motivation will be different. If he is a lover, the motivation may be different. If he is a scientist, the motivation may be still different.

What his motivation is, why the image is there—just by watching the image, you cannot know the motivation. Motivation is more subtle than the image. Image is a gross thing. It is there on the other's mind's screen, you can see it, but why is it there? Why in the first place did it happen? Why is the other thinking about the moon? He may be a painter, a poet—a lunatic. Just by looking in the image, you don't become aware of the motivation. For motivation, you will have to go still deeper in you.

The motivation is known only when you attain to

seedless samadhi, not before it, because motivation is so subtle. It has no image, nothing visible; it is the invisible desire into the deep unconscious of the man. When you have become completely aware and your desires have dissolved . . . Look. When your thoughts dissolve, you become capable of reading others' thoughts: when your desires dissolve, you become capable of reading others' desires.

ॐ

> By performing sanyama on the form of the body to suspend receptive power, the contact between the eye of an observer and the light from the body is broken and the body becomes invisible.

You must have heard stories about yogis who can become invisible. Patanjali tries to reduce everything to a scientific law; he says there is no miracle there also. A person can become invisible by a certain understanding of a certain law. What is that law?

Now physics says if you are seeing me, you are seeing only because sunrays fall on me and then they move, reflect from me. Those sunrays falling on your eyes, that's why you are seeing me. If there is some way, if I can absorb the sunrays and they don't reflect, you will not be able to see me. You can see only if sunrays come to me. If there is darkness and there are no sunrays coming, you cannot see me. But if I can absorb all the sunrays and nothing is reflected back, you will not be able to see me. You will see only a dark patch.

That's what modern physics also says; that's how we see colours. For example, you are wearing orange; I can see that you are wearing orange. What does it mean? It simply means that your clothes are reflecting the orange ray back. All other rays are being absorbed by your clothes. Only the orange colour ray is being reflected. When you see white, it means all rays are reflected back. White is not a colour; all colours are reflected back. White is all colours together. If you mix all colours they become white, so white is all colours; it is not a colour. And if you are using a black dress, nothing is reflected back; all the rays are being absorbed. That's why your dress looks black. Black is also not a colour; it is no-colour, all rays absorbed. That's why if you use black in a hot country, you will feel tremendously hot. Don't use the colour black and move into the hot sun. You will feel very hot because the black goes on absorbing everything. White is cooler. Just looking at white, a coolness. Using white, you feel cool because nothing is absorbed, everything reflected back.

In India, Jainism has chosen white as their colour because of renunciation—because it renounces all. The white colour renounces all. It gives back everything, absorbs nothing. Death is depicted everywhere as black because it absorbs everything. Nothing comes out of it, everything dissolves into it and disappears. It is a black hole. The devil is depicted everywhere as black, evil is depicted everywhere as black, because it is not capable of renouncing anything. It is too possessive. It cannot give anything: it cannot share.

Hindus have chosen orange as their colour for a certain reason, because red rays are reflected back. The red ray entering the body creates sexuality, violence. Red is the colour of violence, of blood. The red ray entering the body creates violence, sexuality, passion, disturbance. Now the scientists say that if you are left in a room coloured completely red, within seven days, you will go mad. Just nothing else is needed; just seeing red things continuously for seven days. Everything red—curtains, the furniture. Everything red, the walls. Within seven days, you will go mad; the red will be too much. Hindus have chosen red, and shades of red—orange, ochre, and others—because they help you to become less violent. The red ray is reflected back; it doesn't enter into the body.

Patanjali says that a man can become invisible if he can absorb all the rays that fall on him. You will not be able to see him. You may be able to see just an emptiness, black emptiness, but the man will become invisible. How does it happen to a yogi? Sometimes it happens. Sometimes it happens and the yogi is unaware of it. Let me explain to you the mechanism of it.

In Patanjali's system of thought, there is a deep correspondence between the outer world and the inner. It has to be; they are together. There is light; from the sun comes the light. Your eyes are receptive to it. If your eyes are not receptive to it, the sun may be there, but you will live in darkness. That's what happens to a blind man—his eyes are not receptive. So your eyes somehow correspond with the sun. In your body, your eyes represent the sun; they are joined together. The sun affects the eyes; the eyes are sensitive towards it. Sound affects your ears. Sound is outside; ears are in you.

The outside reality is known as *tattva*, the element, and the inside correspondence is known as *tanmatra*. In Patanjali's system, these two are very essential to be understood. The *tattva* is the outside reality, the sun, and corresponding to it is something in your eye which he calls *tanmatra*: the essential element inside you. That's why there is a dialogue between the eye and the sun, between the sound and the ear, between the nose and the smell. There is a correspondence, invisible; something is joined and bridged.

When one goes on meditating and comes to understand the gaps, *nirodh*, then accumulates gaps, *samadhi*, then arises one-pointedness, *Ekagrata parinam*; then one can look into the *tanmatras*, the inner elements, the subtle elements. You have seen the sun with the eye, but you have not seen your eye up to now. Only in a deep emptiness one becomes alert and can see his own eye. You have heard the sound, but you have not heard your ear responding to it. The vibration that comes to your ear, the subtle vibration, you have not heard that yet. It is too subtle and you are too gross. You are not yet so refined. You cannot hear that subtle music. You have smelled the rose, but you have not yet been able to smell the subtle element in you which smells the rose, the *tanmatra*.

The yogi becomes capable of listening to the inner sound, which is silence; of seeing the eye, the inner eye, which is pure vision. And there is the mechanism of becoming invisible: *By performing sanyama on the form of the body* . . .

If the yogi just concentrates on his form of the body, his own form of the body, just by that concentration on the form, the sunrays are absorbed in the form and they are not reflected back. When you concentrate on the form, the form opens. All the closed doors open and the sunrays enter into the form and the *tanmatra* of your form absorbs the *tattva* of the sun, and suddenly nobody can see you. Because to see, the light must be reflected.

ॐ

The same happens to sound:

> *This principle also explains the disappearance*
> *of sound.*

When the yogi concentrates on the innermost *tanmatra* of his ear, all sounds are absorbed. And when sounds are absorbed, the very presence of the yogi will give you a certain hunch of silence around you. If you go to a yogi, suddenly you will see you are entering into silence. He creates no sound around him. On the contrary, all the sounds that fall on him are absorbed. And this happens to all his senses. He becomes invisible in many ways.

These are the criteria when you come to meet a yogi. These are the criteria. Not that he is trying to do them. He will not do them; he avoids them. But sometimes they happen. Sometimes sitting with a master . . .

It has happened to many people here; they write to me. Just the other day, there was a question, 'Watching you, what happens? Am I going crazy? Sometimes you disappear.' If you go on watching me, there will be moments when you will see me disappearing. Listening to my words, if you go on concentrating on them, suddenly, you will become aware that they are coming out of silence. And when you feel that, then you have felt me, not before it.

Not that anything is being done. In fact, the yogi never does anything. He simply remains in his being and things go on happening. In fact, he avoids, but still, sometimes, things happen. Miracles follow. There are no miracles, but miracles follow one who has attained to *samadhi*; they go on happening. Like a shadow, they follow the man who has attained to inner space.

This is what I call the science of religion. Patanjali has

laid the foundation. Much has to be done. He has just given the bare structure—much has to be filled in the gaps. It is just a concrete structure. The walls have to be raised, rooms have to be made. You cannot live in a bare, concrete structure. It has yet to be made into a house, but he has given the basic structure.

Five thousand years and the basic structure has remained basic: it has not yet become the abode of man. Man is not ready yet.

Man goes on playing with toys, and the real goes on waiting—waiting that whenever you become mature enough, you will use it. Nobody else is responsible for it; we are responsible. Each human being is responsible for this vast sleepiness that surrounds earth. As I see it, it is like a fog surrounding the whole earth, and man is fast asleep.

I have heard, one day it happened . . .

One very diligent reformist inquired of a man who was staggering blindly drunk along the road, 'You poor man, what drives you to drink this way?'

The happy drunk slurred, 'No one drives me, lady. I am a volunteer.'

Voluntarily, man is in the darkness. Voluntarily, you are in the darkness. Nobody has forced you to be there. This is your responsibility to come out of it. Don't go on blaming Satan and the devil that they have been corrupting you. There is nobody who is corrupting you. It is you. And once you are sleepy, everything that you see is distorted— everything that you touch is distorted, everything that comes in your hands becomes dirty.

Two drunks were walking home along a railway line,

stepping unsteadily from sleeper to sleeper. Suddenly, the one in front said, 'Ah, Trevor, damn it if these aren't the longest flight of stairs I ever did crawl up.'

His friend called back, 'I don't mind the stairs, George, but the low banisters are hell.'

We go on drunk, drunk with ego, drunk with possessions, drunk with things, ignorant of reality; and whatsoever we see is distorted. This distortion creates the world of illusion. The world is not illusory. It is because of our drunk minds the world is illusory. Once our drunkenness disappears, the world shines forth as a tremendously beautiful phenomenon—the world becomes God.

God and the world are not two. They appear as two because we are asleep. Once you are awake, they are one. And once you see the marvellous beauty that is surrounding you, all sadness, all despair, all anguish disappears. Then you live in a totally different dimension of benediction.

Yoga is nothing but a way to look at the world with alert. eyes . . . and the world becomes God. There is no need to search for God anywhere else. In fact, forget about God—just become more alert. In your alertness God is born; in your sleep, he is lost. God is not lost; only you are lost. In your sleep, you forget who you are.

Samadhi is awareness come to its crescendo. *Samadhi* is silence come to flowering. Everyone can attain it because it is everyone's birthright. If you have not claimed it, it is for you. It remains unclaimed, waiting.

Don't waste more time anymore. Use every little bit of life and time that you have for one purpose constantly, that you become more and more aware.

I will tell you one story:

Two Jewish women, Sarah and Amy, met after twenty years. They had been together in college and they had been great friends, but for twenty years they had not seen each other. They hugged each other, they kissed each other.

And Sarah said. 'Amy, how have you been?'

'Just fine. And it is good to see you. How has the world been treating you, Sarah?'

'Would you believe that when Harry and I got married, he took me to a honeymoon three months in the Mediterranean and a month in Israel? What do you think of it?'

'Fantastic,' Amy said.

'We came back home and he showed me the new house that he bought for me—sixteen rooms, two swimming pools, a new Mercedes. What do you think of that, Amy?'

'Fantastic.'

'And now for our twentieth anniversary, he gave me a diamond ring, ten karats.'

'Fantastic.'

'And now we are going to go on a cruise around the world.'

'Oh, that's fantastic.'

'Oh, Amy, I have been talking so fast about what Harry did and has been doing for me. I forgot to ask what your Abe has done for you.'

'Oh, we have had a good life together.'

'But what has he done special?'

'He sent me to charm school.'

'Sent you to charm school? What did you go to charm school for?'

'To teach me how to say "fantastic" instead of "bullshit."'

That's all yoga is all about—to make you aware of the fantastic. It is right by the corner waiting for you, and you are drowned in bullshit. Unhook yourself, loosen yourself out of it. Enough is enough.

And this decision cannot be taken by anybody else. You have to decide. It is your decision the way you are. It is going to be your decision if you want to change and be transformed.

Life is fantastic; only that much can I say to you. And it is just around and you are missing it. There is no need to miss any more.

And yoga is not a belief system. It is a methodology, a scientific methodology how to attain to the fantastic.

ॐ

10. Take the Risk

The question is from Paritosh:

> Since returning to Pune and listening to your discourses, I have been experiencing a certain amount of disquiet. I learn that my ego does not really exist. My greater disquiet now is about my superego, presumably non-existent also, who has been keeping a watchful eye for many years on an ego which is not there; in my dilemma I recall some lines from an anonymous poet. These run something like this:
>
> As I was walking up the stair
> I passed a man who was not there
> He did not come again today.
> I really wish he'd go away.

THE EGO IS the greatest dilemma, and it has to be understood. Otherwise, you can go on and on ad infinitum, creating a new ego fighting with the old.

What exactly is the ego? It is topdogging yourself. It is creating a division in yourself—the division of the topdog and the underdog, the division of the superior and the inferior, the division of the saint and the sinner, the division of good and bad; the division, basically, of God and devil. And you go on getting identified with the beautiful, with the higher, with the superior: and you go on condemning the lower.

If this division exists, then whatsoever you do, there is an ego: you can drop it, and by dropping it, you can create a superego. Then, by and by, the superego will start creating trouble for you, because all division is misery. Nondivision is bliss: division is misery. It will create new problems, new anxieties. Then again you can drop the superego and you can create a supersuperego—ad infinitum, you can go on. And this is not going to solve the problem. You are simply shifting it. You are simply forcing it back. You are trying to avoid the problem.

I have heard about one Catholic who was a fanatic believer in the Virgin Mary and God and the Catholic theology. Then he got fed up, and then he dropped it and he became an atheist; and then he started saying, 'There is no God, and Mary is his mother.' Now the same old thing, and it has become even more absurd.

I have heard about a Jew, a very simple man, a tailor in a small town. One day he was not found in the temple. It was a religious day, and he had always been there, but lately rumours were spreading in the town that he has become an atheist. So the whole town was agog. It was a great event: the tailor has turned atheist. It has never happened in that town; nobody has ever turned atheist. So the whole town went to the tailor's shop. They asked him, but he didn't say anything. He remained silent.

Another day, they again approached him, because it became almost impossible to do anything in the town. The whole town was concerned about the tailor—why has he become an atheist? So they made a deputation, and the shoemaker of the town, who was a little aggressive, became the leader. They came to the tailor's shop, and the shoemaker went to him and asked, 'Have you become an atheist?'

The tailor simply said, 'Yes, I have become an atheist.'

They could not believe their ears. They were not hoping that he would give such an outright answer, so they said, 'Then why did you remain quiet yesterday?'

He said, 'What! What do you mean! Should I accept that I have become an atheist on the day of the sabbath?'

Even if you become an atheist, your old pattern continues.

I have heard about one atheist who was dying. The priest had come, and the priest said to the atheist, 'Now, this is time. Make peace with your God.'

The atheist opened his eyes, said, 'Thank God that I am an atheist.'

It continues. You remain almost the same; only labels change.

Please, try to understand the ego. Don't create a superego. Just try to understand what this ego is.

Ego is a separation from the whole: thinking of yourself that you are separate from the whole. It is just a thought, not a reality. Just a fiction, not a truth. It is just a dream that you have created around yourself. You are not separate from the whole. You cannot be, because once you are separate, you cannot exist. Then the life energy goes on flowing in you, whether you think you are separate or not.

The whole doesn't bother about it. It goes on feeding and nursing you. It goes on 'fuelling' you.

But your idea that you are separate creates many anxieties in its wake. Once you think you are separate from the whole, immediately, you create a division inside also. All that is natural in you becomes inferior—because it seems to belong to the whole. Sex becomes inferior because it seems to belong to the organic unity of the whole.

That's why all religions go on condemning sex. And I say to you, unless sex is totally accepted, nobody can become really religious, because religion is the transformation of the same energy. It is not a denial; it is a deep acceptance. Yes, it is a transformation. But transformation comes through deep acceptance. Nature accepted becomes totally different. Nature denied, and everything goes sour and bitter in you; and then you create hell.

The ego is always happy to condemn something because only by condemnation can you feel superior.

I was reading; it happened:

Once in a church, the vicar in the pulpit said, 'Stand up all who sinned last week.' Half the congregation stood up. Then he said, 'Stand up those who would have sinned if they had had the chance.' The remainder of the congregation stood up.

A woman whispered to her husband, 'It looks as if the vicar is the only good person here.'

The bloke said, 'Don't you believe it. He stood up before any of us.'

The superego, which goes on condemning: the superego,

which goes on telling you this is sin, this is evil, this is wrong, this is bad, is itself the only evil in the world, the only sin. So what to do? You can start condemning ego itself: then you will create a superego. Drop condemnation—*all* condemnation—and ego disappears without creating any superego in the wake. Drop all condemnation.

Who are you to judge? Who are you to say what is right and what is wrong? Who are you to divide existence in two? Existence is one—one organic unity. It is all one: day and night—one: good and bad—one. These divisions are of the ego, of man, they are man-made. Just don't condemn.

If you condemn, you will go on creating something or the other. Stop condemning and see you will find there is no ego left. So ego is not the real problem. The real problem is condemnation, judgement, division. Forget about the ego, because whatsoever you will do with the ego, will create another ego.

There are as many egos as there are persons. Somebody has a very worldly ego, and then somebody has a very religious ego. Somebody goes on saying how much he possesses, and then somebody says how much he has renounced.

A so-called saint was dying, and the disciples had gathered. Those were the last moments, and they were talking near the bed, talking about their master. Somebody said, 'Never again will there be a man who was so moral.' Then somebody else said, 'I have learned much. I have never come across a man who knows so much. We will miss him for ever and ever.' Then somebody else said something else: somebody said that he has renounced the whole world:

and this way they were talking, talking about their master who was going to die. They talked about his knowledge, they talked about his renunciation, they talked about his ascetic ways, they talked about his disciplined character: and then the dying master opened his eyes and he said, 'Nobody is saying anything about my humbleness?'

Then humbleness becomes the ego. Then humility becomes the garb of the ego. Then ego becomes pious. And when any poison becomes pious, it becomes more poisonous.

So if you understand me rightly, please don't start condemning the ego. Otherwise you will create a superego, and then you will feel a disquiet because divided, continuously topdogging yourself, how can you be at ease? Drop condemnation. Stop topdogging yourself. Accept as you are. Not only accept, welcome. Not only welcome, rejoice in it. And suddenly you *will* see there is no ego, there is no superego. They have never been there. You were creating them: you were the creators of them.

Man has created only one thing, and that is ego. Everything else is created by God.

ॐ

> *I move in meditation and work and love but keep feeling it is not enough. Osho, I want you to destroy me once and for all.*

This is from Anand Bodhisattva. Any experience, any experience whatsoever, is not going to be enough. The experience of work, the experience of love, even the experience of meditation, or call it the experience of God; no experience is going to be enough because all experiences are outside you. You remain hidden behind the experience. You are the witness. Experience is happening to you, but you are not it. So whatsoever the experience, no experience will ever be total because the experiencer, the one who is experiencing, is always greater than the experience. And the difference between the experience and the experiencer always remains—the gap—and that gap goes on saying, 'Yes, something is happening but not enough. More is needed.'

That is the misery of the human mind. That's why the mind goes on asking for more, more, more. You earn money and the mind says, 'More.' You make a house; the mind says, 'Make bigger.' You create a kingdom, and the mind says, 'A bigger kingdom is needed.' Then you start meditating, and the mind says, 'Not enough. There are many more peaks to be attained.' And this will remain so because it is something in the very nature of the experience that the experience can never be total.

Then what can be total? Then what can be fulfilling? Remain a witness; don't be lost in the experience. Don't be lost. Just remain alert. Know that this is a passing mood: it will pass. Good or bad, beautiful or ugly, happy or unhappy—a cloud passing by: you remain silent, watching it. Don't get identified with it. Otherwise, love will not fulfil, neither meditation, because, in fact, what is meditation? Meditation is not an experience: it is to become aware of the witness. Just look. Just watch, and remain centred in the watcher, and then anything is total. Otherwise, nothing is total. Then everything and anything is fulfilling: otherwise, nothing is fulfilling.

If you remain a witness, just taking a bath, a shower, is so fulfilling that you cannot expect more. Just taking your breakfast is so fulfilling. Just sipping tea is such a tremendous delight, you cannot think, you cannot imagine, that more is possible. Then each moment becomes a diamond unto itself, and each experience becomes a flowering—but you remain alert. You are not lost in the experience: you don't get identified with it.

I can understand, Bodhisattva. You are trying hard. You are working, meditating. You are doing whatsoever a man can do. More you cannot do. Even if you can do more, that is not going to help. Now the point has come to understand: be the witness. Let experiences pass. Let them come and go. Don't be distracted by them. Don't be pulled in by them. Remain alert, unconcerned—just watching the traffic, watching the clouds in the sky. Be a watcher and suddenly you will see small things have become deep fulfilments—just a small bird singing, or just a small flower opening.

There is a haiku of Baso. In Japan, there flowers a very small flower, nazuna. It is so small and so common and so ordinary and so poor that nobody talks about it. Poets talk about roses. Who talks about a nazuna? It is a gross flower. In many languages there is no name for it because who bothers to name it? People pass by; nobody looks at it. The day Baso attained his first satori, he came out of his cottage and he saw a nazuna flowering. And he says in his haiku, 'For the first time I saw the beauty of a nazuna. It is tremendous. All paradises put together are nothing.'

How did a nazuna become so beautiful? And Baso says, 'It was always there, and I had passed it millions of times, but I had not seen it before'—because Baso was not there. The mind sees only that which can be fulfilling to the ego. Who bothers about a nazuna? It is in no way fulfilling. A lotus is okay, a rose will do, but a nazuna, an ordinary gross flower, so poor, so beggarly, needs nobody's attention, attracts nobody, calls nobody . . . But that day, that morning, the sun rising, and Baso saw a nazuna; he says, 'For the first time I encountered the reality of a nazuna'— but that happened only because he had encountered his own reality.

The moment you have become a witness—that's what *satori* is, *samadhi* is—the moment you have become a witness, everything takes a different colour. Then ordinary green is no longer ordinary green; it becomes extraordinarily green. Then nothing is ordinary. When you are a witness, everything becomes extraordinary, superb.

Jesus says to his disciples, 'Look at the lily in the field.' An ordinary lily flower—it is not ordinary for Jesus, because Jesus is in a totally different space. The disciples must have wondered why he is talking about the lily, what is there to talk about. But Jesus said, 'Even Solomon in all his glory was nothing, in all his splendour was nothing before this flower lily.' Even Solomon. Solomon is the richest, the greatest emperor of Jewish myth—even he was nothing. Before this ordinary lily? Jesus must have seen something which we are missing.

What has he seen? If you become a witness, the world opens all its mysteries to you. Then I say everything is fulfilling.

Somebody asked a great Zen master, 'After you attained your *satori*, what have you been doing?' He said, 'Chopping wood, carrying water. When hungry eating, when tired sleeping.' Everything is beautiful. Chopping wood, carrying water from the well . . .

Just think. Just contemplate a little.

Nikos Kazantzakis in his novel on St. Francis has St. Francis talk to an almond tree. St. Francis comes, the almond tree is there, and St. Francis says, 'Sister, sing me something about God.' And the almond tree blossomed. That's the way the almond tree sings about God. It blossoms in your garden also, but you are not there to say to it, 'Sister, sing of God. Say something about God.' A St. Francis is needed. The almond tree goes on blossoming in our garden also. A thousand and one flowers blossom in your life, but you are not there.

Come back home, become a witness, and then everything—work, love, meditation—everything is a fulfilment. Everything is so total, so infinitely total, that the idea of more simply disappears; and when your mind is not concerned about the more, then you start living, never before it.

I understand your anxiety—*I want you to destroy me, Osho, once and for all.* If I can do it, I would have done it already. If it is only up to me, then I will not wait for you. I will not even ask your permission. But it is not up to me. You have to cooperate. In fact, I am just an excuse—you have to do it.

And don't be in a hurry: don't be impatient. Great patience is needed. But in the West, impatience has become part of the mind. People have forgotten the beauty of patience.

I was reading an anecdote:

The doctor was explaining the new recovery technique to his patient.

'You should begin walking as soon as possible after the operation. On the first day, you must walk around for five minutes, the second day, for ten minutes, and on the third day, you must walk for a full hour. Do you understand?' 'Yes, doctor,' said the apprehensive patient, 'but is it all right if I lie down during the operation?'

Become a little more patient. You are on the operation table. Please rest and cooperate with me because this is not an operation which can be done in your unconsciousness. This is not an operation where anaesthesia can be given to you. The whole operation has to be done when you are conscious. In fact, the more conscious you are, the more easily it can be done—because the whole surgery is of consciousness. I cannot do it against you: I cannot do it without your cooperation. I cannot do it unless you are totally with me.

In fact, you yourself do it by being totally with me: I am just an excuse. The day it will happen, you will understand that I have not done it, you have done it yourself. I have only given you a little confidence to do it. I have only given you a promise that it is possible. I have only given you an assurance that you are not going astray, that you are on the right path, that's all.

In this operation, the patient is the surgeon also. The surgeon stands by the side. Just his presence is helpful— you don't feel afraid, you don't feel alone.

And it *is* good that nobody else can do it to you because if somebody else can make you free, your freedom will not be a real freedom. If somebody else can make you free, somebody else can make you a slave again. Nobody can make you free. Freedom is your choice. That's why it is ultimate, then nobody can take it away from you. If it can be given, it can be taken away. Because it cannot be given, it cannot be taken away.

I cannot really help you. If you want, you can take all the help that is possible through me. Let me explain it to you.

I cannot help because I cannot be positively aggressive towards you. I cannot kill you, but through me, you can commit suicide. You get it? Through me, you can commit suicide: I cannot kill you. I am available. You can help yourself through me. And the day it will happen, you will understand, only then, that you could have done it even alone, but right now it is almost impossible to do it alone. Even with me, it is so difficult to do it.

Don't be impatient, wait, and get more and more in tune with your witnessing self.

It is very easy when there is pain, suffering, not to get identified, but the real problem arises when you are deep in love, happy, blissful, deep in meditation, ecstatic. Then it is very difficult not to get identified, but there hangs the whole thing. That is the very core. Remember it, when you feel blissful: then too remain alert that this too is a mood; it comes and goes. The cloud has come: it will pass. It is a beautiful cloud. Thank it, thank God, but let it remain separate. Don't rush and don't become one with it. In that identification, the idea of more arises.

If you can remain aloof, a watcher on the hill, unconcerned, the idea of more does not arise. Why? Because when the watcher becomes identified with the experience, it becomes mind, and mind is a desire for more. When the watcher remains just a watcher and the experience *there*, just outside passing like a cloud, there is no mind.

Between the two, there is a space; no bridge. In that unbridged state, there is no desire for more—there is no desire at all. One remains fulfilled. One remains absolutely content.

It is on the way, Bodhisattva. Don't be in a hurry and don't be impatient.

❦

I have a belief that in order to grow, I have to take risks, and in order to take risks, I have to make decisions. Then when I try to make decisions, I am filled with anxiety that I will make a wrong choice, as if my life depended on it. What is this craziness?

This seems still to be a belief, not an understanding. Belief is not going to help. Belief means borrowed; belief means you have not understood it yet. You may have become fascinated with it, you may have seen people who have risked and grown through it, but you have still not realized that risk is the only way to live; there is no other way. Not to risk is the only wrong there is; to risk is never wrong.

You cannot risk wrongly because if you are always afraid not to risk, something may go wrong, then you are not risking at all. If everything is guaranteed and then you risk, and everything is settled that everything is right, then you risk—then where is the risk? No, in the risk, the possibility to go wrong; that's why it is a risk. And it is beautiful to move in that openness where something can be right, something can be wrong.

One grows through it because even if you commit a wrong, you will never be the same again. Through committing it, you will understand much. Even if you go astray, you can come back the moment you realize it. And when you come back, you have learned something—and learned the hard way. Not just memorized, it has become part of your blood, bones, and marrow. So never be afraid of going astray. People who are afraid of going astray, they become paralyzed. They never move.

And life is risk because life is alive; it is not dead. Only in a grave is there no risk. When you are dead, there is no risk.

One disciple asked Lao Tzu, 'Is it not possible to be at ease, comfortable in life?'

Lao Tzu said, 'Wait. Soon you will die, and in the grave you can be at ease and comfortable forever and forever—for eternity.'

Don't waste life for that, because that is coming. These few moments live. And there is no other way to live; to live means to risk. It is always there. It has to be so because you are a flow. You can go astray.

I have heard about a man who was always afraid of deciding, but one has to decide. So he had to decide, and whatsoever he would decide, would always go wrong, and it had become almost a part of his life. And he knew it, that whatsoever he decided, will go wrong. The business will bring no profit; the train that he decides to go on, he will miss; the woman that he decides to marry will fall in love with somebody else. He was always missing.

One day it happened, he had to go to another town for some business work and there was only one airline and only one plane—there was no question of decision. So he was very happy because there is no question of decision; there is no alternative. He had to take that plane. But just in the middle, the engines failed.

He was very much worried; he said, 'My God! This time I have not decided. There was no alternative. Now this is too much. If something is wrong with me and my decision, it's okay, but this time I have not decided at all. You have decided.' He was a follower of St. Francis, so he called, 'St. Francis, save me! At least this time. I have never asked your help because I was always deciding, so I knew it was because something is wrong with me that everything goes wrong. This time I am not at fault.'

A hand from the sky came and took him out of the plane. He was very happy. Then a voice was heard in the sky, 'Which Francis? Francis Xavier, or Francis of Assisi? Tell me whom you have called!'

Now again . . . You cannot escape. Life is always a risk. One has to choose. Through choice you grow, through choice you become mature. Through choice, you fall and you get up again.

Don't be afraid of falling, otherwise your legs will lose the capacity to move. Nothing is wrong in falling. Falling is part of walking; falling is part of life. Fall, get up again, and every fall will make you stronger: and every time you go astray, you will come back better, more experienced, more aware. Next time the same path will not be able to distract you. Commit as many errors as you can—only don't commit the same error again and again.

Nothing is wrong in committing errors. Commit as many as you can—the more you can, the better, because the more experience, the more awareness will come to you. Don't remain sitting, don't remain hanging in an indecisive state of mind. Decide! Not to decide is the only wrong decision because then you are missing everything.

It is said about Thomas Edison that he was working on some project and he failed one thousand times. For almost three years he worked continuously, and he would fail. He tried everything, nothing seemed to work. His disciples became desperate, hopeless. One day one disciple said, 'You have done one thousand experiments. Every experiment has failed. We seem not to be moving anywhere.' Edison looked surprised; he said, 'What are you saying? What do you mean? Not moving anywhere? One thousand wrong doors are closed: now the right door cannot be very far away. We have committed one thousand errors; that much we have learned. What do you mean by saying that we are wasting our time? These one thousand errors cannot attract us anymore. We are coming, we are zeroing upon the truth. How long can it escape?'

Never be afraid of errors, mistakes, of going wrong.
This question is from Prem Nisha. She is always afraid. She is so much afraid she sits somewhere hiding; I can never see her. Maybe just my look and there may be a risk. She goes on hiding herself. I know she is there, every day she is there, but she sits in such a way, somewhere behind the pillar, that I cannot see her. Or even sometimes she is in front of me, she sits with her head so bent down that I cannot recognize where she is.
Life is moving. You can remain sitting: then your life will be like a death. Get up and be moving. Take the risk.

Her situation is like a little boy:
Wise Winifred returned from his summer camp with

awards for woodcraft, hiking and sailing; and also with a small star. Asked what the star was for, he replied, 'For having my trunk packed neatly when we came home.' His mother was very pleased until Winifred added, 'I had not unpacked it.'

Nisha, unpack! Don't be afraid that you may not be able to pack it again so neatly. A little mess is good; nothing is wrong about it. But remaining with unopened life, closed, is the only wrong you can do to life. That is refusal. That is refusing God. The whole has created you to live here, to live as profoundly as possible—to live as dangerously as possible. The whole wanted you to be so alive, alive at the peak—wildly alive—that's why you are sent. And you are afraid something may go wrong.

God is not afraid in sending you. He is not afraid. He goes on sending all sorts of people—good people, wrong people, saints and sinners. He goes on. He is not afraid. If He was afraid, the world would have disappeared long before, or it would never have come into existence. If He was afraid, 'If I create people and they do something wrong, if man goes astray . . .' In fact, the first man, Adam, went astray. Man has to go that way. He created the first man, and he rebelled and disobeyed and he took the risk of getting out of the comfort of the garden of Eden, of the convenience. He took the dangerous path. Just think of Adam—what risk. And God has not stopped since then. Otherwise, He would have stopped. There is no need. He created the first man, and the first man went astray—now no need. He goes on creating.

In fact, it seems that God created the whole situation. He said to Adam, 'Don't eat the fruit of this tree.' This was temptation. Christians are absolutely wrong when they say that the devil tempted Adam, absolutely wrong. God tempted when he said, 'Don't eat the fruit of this tree of knowledge.' What more temptation can you imagine? Just try with any child. Tell him not to go into that room, and the next thing that he is going to do is to go into that room.

Just a small sanyasi, Dheeresh, was going back to London. I gave him a box and told him not to open it. He said, 'Yes, I will not open it.' And then I talked to his mother, and again I told him, 'Remember not to open it.' He said, 'I will never open it.' The mother said, 'He has already opened it!'

It is God who tempted. When He said to Adam, 'Don't eat the fruit of this tree,' there is no need for any devil. God is the greatest tempter because He wants you to go, to experience, to move all over existence. Even if you go astray, you cannot go out of Him. Where can you go? Even if you do wrong, what wrong can you do, because He is and only He is? You cannot do anything against Him. There is no possibility. It is just a game of hide-and-seek. God sends you, gives you a temptation—because that is the only way to grow.

Yes, you will come back someday. Adam goes out of the garden; Jesus comes back. Jesus is Adam coming back. It is the return; the return journey. Jesus is Adam who has realized, who has become aware of the error, of the mistake; but Jesus is not possible if there is no Adam in the beginning.

A priest was talking to small children and he was telling them how to pray to God, how your mistakes can be forgiven. Then he asked questions, he asked, 'To be forgiven, what is the basic requirement?' A small child stood and said, 'To sin.'

To commit a mistake: to be forgiven, that's a must. Adam is needed for Jesus to be. Adam is the beginning of going astray: Jesus is coming back.

But Jesus is totally different from Adam. Adam was innocent. Jesus is wise—innocent plus something more. That plus has come to him because he went astray. Now he knows more, understands the ways of life and growth more.

Everybody has to enact this drama again and again. You have to be Adam to become a Jesus. Don't be worried. Take courage. Don't be a coward. Move.

And I tell you even going astray is all right. Just don't do the same mistake again and again, that's enough—because if you do the same mistake again, again, then you are stupid. If you never do the mistake, you are worse than stupid. If you do new mistakes every day, you will become wise. Wisdom comes through experience, and you cannot have it in any other way. There is no short cut to it.

'I have a belief that in order to grow, I have to take risks . . .' Drop this belief. It is not a question of belief. Watch life; watch yourself. Let this become an insight, not a belief. Not that I say so that you believe, but try to understand that you will remain crippled if you are afraid and you don't move. If a child is afraid and does not try to walk . . . And everybody knows he will fall many times—he may have wounds, he may hurt himself—this is going to happen; but that's the only way to learn. By and by, he learns how to balance. Watch a child trying to walk.

First, he moves on all fours, then he tries the greatest adventure of standing on two feet.

I call it the greatest because the whole of humanity has come out of that adventure. Animals go on moving on four: only man has tried two. Animals move with more safety. Man has been a little fascinated, more fascinated, with danger—he tried to move on two.

Just think of the first man who must have stood on two feet. He must have been one of the most unorthodox, nonconformist of men—the greatest revolutionary, the rebel—and everybody would have laughed at the ridiculousness of it. Just think when everybody was walking on all fours and, suddenly, one man stood on two feet: the whole society must have laughed. They must have said, 'What? . . . what are you doing? Have you gone mad? Nobody has ever walked on two. You will fall; you will break your bones. Come down, come back to the old way.' And it is good that man never listened to them. They must have laughed. They must have tried in every way to put him back in the old fold, but he moved.

Those conservatives are still in the trees. The monkeys, the baboons—they are the conservatives, the Tories. The revolutionary has become man. They are still clinging to the trees and moving on all fours. They may be still thinking, 'And why have these people gone wrong? What misfortune has befallen them?'

But if you try something new, you become available to something new at the same moment, instantly. Don't be afraid. Move, in the beginning, small steps, small decisions, remaining always aware that something is always possible, you may go wrong. But what is wrong in being wrong? Come back. You will come more wise.

Don't let it be just a belief. Let it become an understanding. Only then does it become effective.

'. . . and in order to take risks I have to make decisions'. Of course, one has to make decisions. That is one of the most beautiful things in life. That shows that you are free. You would have liked that somebody else decide for you: then you will be slaves. In that way, animals are in a better position—everything is decided. They have fixed food to eat; they have a fixed pattern of life to live. They don't decide themselves; they are never confused.

Man is the only animal who is always confused, but that is his glory because he has to decide. He is always hesitating, always hanging between two alternatives—St. Francis of Assisi, St. Francis Xavier—and always risky. Just think of that man. If that hand is from St. Francis of Assisi and he says St. Francis Xavier—gone. But one has to decide. Through decision, your soul is born; you become integrated.

Decide, whatsoever your decision. Don't go on remaining indecisive. If you are indecisive, you will always be doing something contradictory. You will be moving in both the ways together, simultaneously—because indecisive, also, you have to live. 50 per cent you will be going towards the north, 50 per cent towards the south. Then there is misery, anguish, suffering.

A man rushed into the income-tax office and grasped the manager by the lapels. 'Look, I am in a bit of a state. My wife has disappeared,' he said.

'Has she?' said the inland revenue officer. 'That's unfortunate, I guess, but this is the taxation department.

You ought really to inform the police.'

The man shook his head earnestly and replied, 'I know. I am not being caught like that again. The last time she went, I told the police, and they found her.'

Then why go at all to report to the income-tax officer? But part says something has to be done, the wife has disappeared; the husband has to do something. Another part feels happy and says, 'Good that she has disappeared. Don't go to the police station; they may find her again.'

This is how life goes on—half/half—and then you become fragmentary. The husband, the respectable husband, has to do something; and the man, who needs freedom, has to do something else. He is happy that the wife is gone. The husband looks sad—or pretends to be sad—shows his misery, is afraid that because of the inner man, people may become aware that he is feeling happy. That will not be good: that will be shattering to the respectable ego. So he has to do something. He cannot go to the police station: then he goes somewhere else.

Watch your life. Don't waste your life that way.

Decision is needed. You have to decide each moment. Each moment lost without decision creates fragmentariness in you. Each moment decided, by and by, you become collected, one piece, you become together. A moment comes, you become integrated. Decision is not really the thing: decisiveness. Through decisions you become decisive.

It happened once:

A terrified young woman patient went to the dentist and sat in the waiting room. She had her sister with her to look after the three-month-old baby. Soon it was her turn to go into the torture chamber.

As she sat in the operating chair, she said nervously to the dentist, 'I don't know which is the worst—to have a tooth taken or to have a baby.'

The dentist said, curtly, 'Well, make your mind up quickly, please. I have got a lot of other people waiting.'

And I would like to say that to Nisha also. She has been hanging around here. Make up your mind. Decide. Just hanging around is not good. Either be here or be somewhere else, but be. If you want to be here, be here, but then be totally here. Then this place becomes your whole world and this moment becomes your whole eternity. Or don't be here, but don't go on hanging. Be somewhere else, that too is good. Then be there. It is not a question of where you are. The question is, 'Are you there?' Don't remain divided. Don't go on moving in all directions; otherwise you will go mad.

Surrender is a decision, the greatest decision there is. To trust somebody is a decision. The risk is there. Who knows? The man may be just deceiving. You fall in love with a woman; you trust. You fall in love with a man; you trust. Who knows? In the night, the man may murder you. Who knows? The wife may escape with all your bank balance. But one risks: otherwise love is not possible.

Hitler never allowed any woman to sleep in his room. Even his girlfriends were never allowed. He would see them in the day, but in the night, not in the room. He was so afraid. Who knows? The girl may poison him, strangle him in the night. Just think, the misery of such a man. He cannot even trust a woman. What a life he must have led, a life of hell. Not only did he live in hell, all those who were around him lived in hell.

It is reported that he was talking to a British diplomat on the seventh storey of his building, and he was trying to impress upon the British diplomat that there was no use in resisting him, simply surrender; and he said, 'We are going to win the world. Nobody can prevent us.' One soldier was standing there. Just to give an example, he said, 'Jump out of the window.' The soldier simply jumped—out of a window, seven storeys high. The British diplomat could not believe it. The soldier didn't even hesitate. And then to make the point even more clear, he said to another soldier, 'Jump!' and the other jumped. Now this was too much. And to make the point go exactly to the heart of the diplomat, he said to the third soldier, 'Jump!'

But by that time, the diplomat had become afraid and shocked; he took hold of the man, the soldier who was going to jump. He said, 'Wait! Why are you so ready to commit suicide? Why are you so unhesitant to leave your life?'

The man said, 'Leave me alone! You call this life?' And he jumped.

Hitler lived in a hell and he created a hell for others also—'You call this life?'

If love is not there, life is not possible. Life deeply means love: love deeply means life. Love is a trust, a risk.

To be near me is to be tremendously in love because that is the only way to be near me. I am not here just trying to propagate some teachings. I am not a teacher. I am giving you a different vision of life. It is risky: I am trying to convince you that the way you have lived up to now is basically wrong; there is another way—but of course that other way is unknown, is in the future. You have never tasted it. You will have to trust me; you will have to move with me in the dark. The fear will be there: the danger will be there. It is going to be painful—all growth is—but through pain one reaches to ecstasy. Only through pain is ecstasy reached.

✍

> *During meditation, I invoke your emptiness and I find that gradually your emptiness pervades over me. Can I, by this method, imbibe your total being? Will I be able to invoke you totally in me? Please bless me. (You may not even reply verbally.)*

I am never replying, ever, only verbally. Whenever I am replying to you, the reply is two-dimensional. It is on two planes together. One is the verbal: that is for those who cannot understand any other dimension—that is for the deaf and the blind and the dead. Then, simultaneously, on another plane there is a non-verbal communication; that is for those who can hear, who can see, who are alive.

And never ask for my blessings, because they are always there, whether you ask for them or not. Whether you cooperate with me or not, whether you are for me or against, that does not make any difference to my blessings. My blessing is not an act. It is just like breathing; it is always there. If you can feel, you will find it always there. I am my blessings.

And you have stumbled upon a right method: *During meditation, I invoke your emptiness and I find that gradually your emptiness pervades over me. Can I, by this method, imbibe your total being?* Yes, absolutely yes. Go on, don't be afraid, because emptiness will sooner or later give you a deep fear—because emptiness means death. Emptiness means you are disappearing, and before your reality opens, you will have to be gone from there completely. You will have to be absent before you can feel the presence of your reality. Before you can feel the fullness of being, you will have to become absolutely empty. There is a gap—you become absolutely empty, *almost*. There is a small gap and that gap is deathlike. You are gone and God has not entered yet, just a small interval, but that small interval looks like infinity.

In a court there was a case, a murder case, but the jurors and the judge were going to decide that the man is innocent. Because there were reliable witnesses who said that only for three minutes had he gone out and then he was again back amidst them. Only for three minutes was he not there with them, and it seems too much to commit a murder in three minutes. Then the lawyer from the opposite party said, 'Let me try one experiment.' He took his pocket-watch out and he said, 'Now, everybody should close his eyes and remain silent. After three minutes, I will give you a hint that three minutes are over.' Everybody remained silent.

If you remain silent for three minutes, three minutes is long, very long; they last very long. They appear very long, non-ending. Have you ever stood—somebody dies, a political leader or somebody, and you have to stand for one minute in silence. That one minute looks so long that you start thinking that this political leader should not have died.

Three minutes . . . and after three minutes were over,

the lawyer said, 'I have nothing else to say.' And the jurors decided that this man had committed the murder. They changed their verdict. Three minutes are so long.

Whenever you are silent, one moment of silence will be very, very long. And it is impossible to imagine what happens when you are absent, a single moment may be the gap, but it looks almost like eternity. One gets very much afraid. One wants to go back, to hold to the past.

Soon that fear will arise. Remember that time, don't be afraid. Don't go back; don't fall back. Move on. Accept death, because only out of death, the life abundant. Only when you die, you attain to the deathless.

It is always there waiting for you. It is not something outside you; it is your very core of being, the deathless. But you are identified with the mortal, with the body, with the mind. These are momentary, changing. Somewhere within you there is pure consciousness, untouched, uncorrupted. That pure consciousness is your real nature.

The whole yoga is an effort to reach to that purity of being, to that virginity and out of that virgin, Jesus is born. Once you have touched that virginity in you, you are reborn; it is a resurrection.

Let me be your death so that you can be reborn again. A master is a death and a life, a cross and a resurrection. You have stumbled upon an exactly right method. Now go ahead. Imbibe that emptiness more and more, become empty. Soon, everything changes—emptiness disappears. First everything else disappears and emptiness gathers inside you, then, when the emptiness is total, it also disappears.

Buddha used to say to his disciples, about this phenomenon, 'It is as if you burn a candle in the evening.' The whole night the candle goes on burning; the flame burns the candle, the stuff of the candle. The flame goes on burning it. The candle goes on disappearing, disappearing, disappearing . . . By the morning, the candle has disappeared. The last moment, when the candle has completely disappeared, the flame jumps and is gone. First it destroys the candle, then it itself is gone.

The same happens, first, if you try to imbibe emptiness, nothingness, egolessness, it will destroy everything else. It will remain like a flame, destroying everything. When everything is destroyed and you are completely empty, a jump of the flame, and emptiness is also gone. Suddenly, you are back home, fulfilled, overflowing. That's where a man becomes a god.

⚕